I0464117

How to Buy Unlimited
Investment Properties

Mark Reister

Published by Nameless Books
an imprint of Hourigan SA
Victoria, Mahé, Seychelles

Set in Linux Libertine

Find the author online:
professionalsshepparton.com.au

2013.02.17

About the author

I first became interested in real estate when I sold my second home in Perth, WA. It was a positive experience and I made a bit of money from the sale. After returning to my native home state of Victoria, I pursued a career as an estate agent and in 1993 I began with a large and highly respected company, Woodards Real Estate. It was an incredibly steep learning curve, as I'd never sold anything before, but with the help of some great work colleagues and mentors I made a living.

I met the love of my life and now wife Trudie while vacationing overseas. We live in Shepparton, which is a small regional city approximately two hours' drive north of Melbourne, with our two children Chloe and Liam.

As a result of the move north, I left Woodards Real Estate after working there for almost seven years. I had a brief break from selling real estate, but my love of real estate has never waned. It was during this break from selling that I became more and more interested in finding out how to buy unlimited investment properties.

I say "unlimited" because during my career as an estate agent I had occasionally met buyers who came back to me year after year wanting to buy another investment property. I started off reading numerous books on the subject and attending investment seminars, but whether it was due to a lack of drive on my part or because the information provided was not specific enough, I never turned that information into an investment portfolio. However, having met people who own large investment portfolios, I knew it was possible.

How to Buy Unlimited Investment Properties is my first book, and won't be my last. It describes exactly how I reached my goals, including all the failures I had along the way.

I am now a part owner of a real estate office, Professionals McNamara, Thompson, Reister. I still love real estate, and will happily talk about the subject with anyone who has a similar interest. I hope you enjoy my first book, and above all that it is beneficial. If you decide to buy investment properties, I hope you reach your goals with a great deal of ease, and that your journey is both rewarding and enjoyable.

—Mark Reister

Contents

This is my story about a journey to reach my goals, which may never have begun if not for the courage and support of my friends Ian, Dean, and Mark, my parents, my brother Dean, and Trudie.

This story involves all these people in important ways, and I dedicate this book to them.

Prologue

Have you ever wondered what sort of people attend investment seminars? Are they battlers striving to make ends meet, or middle class people trying to break into the upper class? Maybe they're members of the upper class, looking for new ways to get even further ahead. They could be academics searching for a course that will enlighten them as to their ideal vocation—one that pays well but requires no work.

Actually, all these kinds of people attend investment seminars.

It seems that every time you look through a major daily newspaper, there are more and more ads promoting these seminars. Some advocate buying shares, while others urge you into property portfolios. Many say you don't need to start with money to get rich, that their strategies are suitable for anyone, easy, and low-risk.

With more and more courses trying to capture the interest of potential investors, the promises made by 'no risk' courses get larger with each new edition of the newspaper. Some offer quick introductory sessions that cost little or nothing, and may last only a few hours. Other, more intensive courses can last weeks, and cost the participants tens of thousands of dollars.

Recently, I attended many property investment seminars, not because of the advertisements, but because I was looking for a new career.

The situations vacant section in the paper was running an ad for someone enthusiastic to help clients build property portfolios. "The successful applicant requires no previous experience, and the expected salary in the first year is $130,000, with potential to increase further," it read.

While the dollar figure excited me, the prospect of working with real estate was appealing in itself. I had worked as an estate agent for six years—far better than "no previous experience"—so I replied to the advertisement and was invited for a job interview.

The position was indeed intended to help people build property portfolios, by showing potential investors how to manipulate the real estate market. A condition of working for this firm was that employees must attend its three-and-a-half-day "Investment Strategy Seminar." The course cost me the equivalent of three months' salary, but it promised me I'd recoup the cost of my course twofold with my first property transaction. I agreed to their terms, and started out on my path to make a fortune—so I hoped.

Before joining my new firm, I'd already read numerous books on investment, and sat through a score of seminars on money, motivation, and setting goals. Some of these courses were held in hotels, some in school lecture theatres, and others in large concert halls. The number of participants at these courses ranged from a handful of people, to about two thousand—the largest course I attended.

Regardless of the size of the course or the venue, the majority of these courses were of some benefit to me. Even if the information rehashed something I'd already heard, having it reinforced usually motivated me. Unfortunately, maybe because I lacked drive or enthusiasm, maybe because the information given out at these seminars wasn't specific enough, I never turned those seminars into a fortune.

As a real estate agent, I'd learned a lot about real estate, but I learned much more by buying and selling my own home. I did this a few times, and each time made a little money, but selling my own houses was more to accommodate my lifestyle and work than to make money. The positive experiences I had in selling my homes helped build my bank balance, but I still needed to live somewhere. So, like many people, I'd use my gains to buy a new, usually larger home.

The problem is, buying a house isn't cheap. Any money that I'd saved went into buying a bigger home than the last, and that bigger home incurred bigger expenses. The money I had in the bank soon disappeared when the new home, complete with a big new mortgage, came along.

But trading the money in my account for a bigger and better house didn't exactly distress me. Isn't this what most people do? Save a bit, buy as expensive a place as they can afford, and then work hard for the next two or three decades paying off the mortgage?

At least I thought I had a good investment that would grow. Twenty-five years later, about the time I was ready to retire, the house would be paid off and I'd own it. I accepted this as a fairly typical financial path. My parents followed it, and so did my friends' parents, and now my friends and I were on it. If I was lucky and discerning with money, but not necessarily frugal, I could have a comfortable middle-class lifestyle.

Certainly, nothing is wrong or even unattractive about this path. My parents are still married after thirty-three years. Dad had a steady income from the factory he worked at for twenty-five years. They raised two healthy boys, and live in a four-bedroom family home in the suburbs. Now in semi-retirement, they enjoy an overseas holiday every couple of years. When I was growing up I never thought of us as rich, but I certainly never thought we were poor. We were comfortable.

I am not sure if it was just out of curiosity, if I wanted to prove to myself that I could do it, but I wanted to know how and why some people had bigger houses, drove foreign cars, had more holidays and seemed more comfortable. Maybe after I'd attended enough investment seminars and read enough books I felt compelled to do something. Or maybe a competitive instinct told me I was as smart as those investment course presenters and could do just as well. Whatever the catalyst, I decided that I wanted to change from the path I was on, to the path taken by people who can afford whatever they want.

The idea behind my new job was to help people build property portfolios that would let them retire with a large passive income and no stress. I had heard that you should only take advice from people who have achieved what you want to achieve. Emulate those people who are where you want to be, I'd heard.

I still hold to this as truth. The problem was that I wasn't yet where I wanted to be, but I was expected to help other people get there anyway. I might

have bought and sold a couple of my own houses, but I wasn't a property mogul, and had never
owned a portfolio of investment properties. So I
decided I'd do better, trying to get rich, by building
my own property portfolio than by telling people
how to do something I'd never done myself.

I *did* do it, in the end, and now I can tell you how.

1. The Valuation

A conservative strategy

After deciding I had to get rich by building my *own* property portfolio if I was going to do it at all, I needed a strategy.

By nature, I am not a gambler. I wanted to proceed with absolute certainty that I would always be able to meet all my financial commitments. So, to test some ideas I had, I experimented with the apartment I was living in.

About six months earlier, in August 2000, I had purchased a two-bedroom, 70m² apartment in the Melbourne CBD. I'd not purchased this property as an investment. I had just returned from living interstate, and wanted to experience inner-city living for the first time. After two weeks looking for apartments in the local newspapers, I happened to drive past an estate agent's "open for inspection" board.

I inspected the property, which was for sale for $225,000. Within half an hour I offered $205,000, and concluded the purchase later that day. It was a newly refurbished warehouse style apartment. Because the property was complete and ready to be occupied immediately, there was no saving on stamp duty, as there would have been if the apartment had been purchased off the plan in Victoria.

You can use the strategies I talk about whether or not you own or have ever purchased a home. Because of my conservative nature, I tested the ideas I'm about to discuss with you using a property I already owned. But even without it, I could have still used these ideas with my parents' house or even a friend's house.

The only financial risk I had to take was to pay for an independent sworn valuation. Such a valuation is prepared by a licensed valuer, and can be done using different methods. Usually, though, the comparison method is used, in which similar properties that have recently sold are used to determine the value of the property being assessed. Very few estate agents are licensed to provide you with a sworn valuation, and unlike estate agents, valuers must provide evidence to support their valuation and can be sued if wrong. You can find a licensed valuer by looking in your local phone book or searching the internet.

If you don't get the result you want with your test case, you don't have to proceed any further than this first step.

The ideal property for such a test will have been purchased within the last twelve months, so that one can compare the valuer's figure to the price that the owner (which may be you) paid. The more recent the purchase, the better.

When I went to get my own valuation, for the apartment I'd bought just six months earlier, I wanted to see if I could make money out of thin air by *creating* new equity in my property. I wanted to test how much I could influence a valuer's thinking, and see if it was possible to convince them to give me a higher valuation for my apartment.

Setting expectations

Before I invited a valuer to inspect my property, I needed to determine what I thought was the highest possible outcome I could achieve. I started by gathering sales results of all properties comparable to my own. I concentrated on two-bedroom apartments sold in the last six months within the CBD.

When choosing properties for comparison, it's best to look within about 3–4km. Choose only properties that have sold in the last six months.

Ignore properties that are still for sale—they may go for significantly less than the asking price, and if that asking price is overly inflated, it may never sell and could be withdrawn from the market. Choose a property that appeals to the same group of people as your own (family home buyers, first home buyers, etc.). The two properties should offer the same number of bedrooms, similar living space and land size. They should be about the same age, and their construction should be the same (both brick, both timber, etc.). Finally, only compare apples with apples. There's no point comparing houses with units, townhouses, flats, or villas. Different types of dwellings appeal to different buyers and can achieve vastly different sales results.

I started gathering sales results by visiting my local estate agents and telling them I considered selling my apartment and therefore wanted to know what they had recently sold that I might use as a comparison. Good estate agents should be able to call upon numerous examples immediately. Because the estate agent wants to win your confidence and ultimately your business, they will be likely to mention only their better sales results.

In addition to the list of addresses and sales prices, I also asked for a copy of the advertising brochure for each property, which usually includes a floor plan. I also gathered sales evidence from results published in local newspapers, and by searching real estate sites on the internet. Many of these sites now have facilities that let you find previous sale results going back as far as six years. This information includes photos, a description of the property, a brochure, and the sale price and date.

As you would expect, when I compared these sales results with the price I paid for my apartment, some properties had sold for more some had sold for less. The cheaper properties I discarded.

To analyze the remaining results, I typed a summary page briefly listing each property:

- its size in square metres (m^2)
- number of bedrooms and bathrooms
- car parking spaces and additional features
- sale price and sale date

To each summary I attached the brochures the estate agents provided.

After reviewing this information to see what sort of prices similar properties had sold for, I set a range that I would be satisfied with in a valuation. First I picked the lowest figure I would accept: $215,000. Then I chose a figure to represent the most optimistic possible estimate: $245,000.

The most likely outcome which was somewhere between these two extremities: between $220,000 and $230,000.

By choosing a range, I opened my mind to the wide variety of possible outcomes, and I could start thinking in advance about what I'd do when the valuation figure became a reality.

Next, I invited three different estate agents to assess my apartment for rental and sales purposes.

I did this for a few reasons. First, if the sworn valuation went well, I intended to rent my apartment and would need rental estimates anyway. But more importantly, high rental estimates can add credibility to your valuation figure.

Just like I wanted a high valuation, I also wanted high rental estimates. To help achieve this, I mentioned to each agent that I would most likely rent my property furnished. The general consensus was that furnishings should increase rent by approximately $100 per week. I requested that the written estimates show the rental figure inclusive of furnishings, but that no reference be made in the letter to furniture. This way, I had a letter showing the maximum rent level possible with no mention of whether furniture was or was not included.

My second reason for inviting estate agents to inspect my apartment was that unlike a sworn valuation, you do not need to pay an estate agent for their opinion of value. As a result, I could afford to get as many opinions as I needed to get the result I wanted. This proved fairly easy. If the estate agent believes you are considering selling your property, and they are competing for your business, their opinion of value is usually on the high side of what you might get if the place is indeed listed for sale.

The third reason was that I wanted to practise my arguments for a higher valuation on estate agents before incurring the cost of a sworn valuer.

Finally, I thought a few high opinions of value from local agents, combined with the sales evidence I had gathered and the rental estimates, would help influence the sworn valuer to give a higher valuation. After all, valuers are just people, and can be influenced by sound, logical arguments. A valuation of any sort is nothing more than one person's opinion based on information available at the time.

In this case, I wanted to provide all the information necessary for the valuer to make an informed decision on the value of my property. The effort I'd gone to in obtaining both rental and sales estimates was to see how far I could push the result.

While I was compiling all this information, I also kept a watchful eye out for newspaper articles telling positive stories about the state of the real estate market. Because journalists like sensational stories, to them the real estate market is always in a state of boom or bust. Usually, though, even during a depressed market you can still find stories of "Record Price Paid in Street", or "Sold Well Above Reserve Price." A perennial lead story is "Numerous Bidders Spur Excellent Clearance Rate." As you'd expect, by now I was only interested in stories with a positive spin on the market. All these articles I added to my mounting data.

If at first you don't succeed...

Armed with my comparable sales evidence, estate agents' estimates, rental estimates and newspaper articles, it was time to get a sworn valuation. Each bank has a panel of approved valuation firms they use just for this purpose. Most large valuation firms appear on the panels of most banks. If I obtained a valuation from a firm not on my bank's panel, the valuation would later be irrelevant. I contacted my bank and obtained a list of their approved valuers. After calling each firm to enquire which banks they can carry out work for, I made an appointment and met a valuer a few days later.

The valuation firm I chose was on the panel of all major banks and numerous second-tier lenders.

By using this firm, I was not restricting my choice of banks for my later financial purposes.

Because my apartment was only 70m², the inspection was over in the time it takes to boil an egg. After he'd inspected my apartment, I asked the valuer what figure he had in mind.

Unfortunately, his opinion and my desired outcome were remote strangers. In the valuer's opinion, my apartment was worth precisely what I paid for it: $205,000. Justifying his estimate, he argued that the real estate market was stable, with no price fluctuations over the previous six-month period.

After initially reeling from the impact, I quickly gathered my thoughts and comparable sales evidence to launch a counterargument for a higher figure. We lunged and parried for a while. The valuer was armed with all the lower comparable sales I had discarded. I wielded my higher-priced comparable sales, but with little effect. His opinion was that because so little time had elapsed since I purchased the property, and because the market was stable, the information I gathered was inconsequential. He dismissed it outright. My passionate counterattack at least won a conciliatory note when he conceded that if I were lucky he might be able to increase my valuation figure by up to $5,000. Disappointingly, my first attempt at obtaining a high sworn valuation was a resounding failure.

At this point, it's important to note that valuers have access to exactly the same information you have. This includes the purchase price you paid for your home. A significant difference is that while you have a vested interest in your property, a valuer does not. As a result, it is worth investing extra effort into finding more comparable sales and collating more data about your property and the real estate market than the valuer has an interest in doing. Since the valuer has no interest in your property, they are usually only too happy to have their work done for them. But you must produce sufficient evidence, backed by logical, rational arguments, to support your case.

...try, try again

Despite my first failure, I still believed I could sway a valuer's opinion to my way of thinking, so I called the second valuation company of my choice, from the list of approved valuers provided by my bank.

It was rather like preparing for a job interview after your first one goes horribly wrong. I reviewed my *modus operandi*. I revisited my list of comparable properties (and made no changes), rehearsed my key arguments for a higher valuation, and re-appraised my approach once the valuer arrived.

I met the second valuer at the apartment, and invited him in as far as the dining room table. This time, I decided to go through all the information first, before letting him walk through. Without asking, I put on the kettle, sat him down and told him that I wanted to show him some information that I thought might help him. Over a coffee and after chatting for about an hour, I invited him to view the rest of the apartment.

He wandered from one end of the apartment to the other in about thirty seconds, a round trip of approximately 20 meters, all without opening a cupboard or measuring a single surface. He then confidently declared that my opinion of value was correct, albeit perhaps somewhat conservative. As you can appreciate, after my first failure at ob-taining a suitable valuation, this comment left me wanting confirmation that I had heard correctly. With a broad grin on my face, I listened intently as he reiterated that in his opinion my assessment of the property's value was correct—his report would show a valuation figure of $245,000.

A more than satisfactory result!

Having purchased the property only six months earlier for $205,000, this valuation already gave me an extra $40,000 equity in the property, which I needed and intended to use to start me on my path to building a property portfolio.

The secret of my success

An important difference between the first and second valuations was the time I took at the start of the second valuation talking to the valuer.

During our chat, I was able to demonstrate that I had a sound knowledge of the real estate market around my apartment and the broader market in general. Significantly, although I had comparable sales, which were much more expensive than my home, I communicated that I was not expecting a valuation figure as high as the one he ultimately delivered. I did this to show that I did not have an unrealistic expectation.

Another and perhaps more important difference between the two valuations was that during the second one I emphasized that I was *not* going to sell my property. Valuers can get into trouble if they provide a valuation figure, and the property owner decides to sell their property on that basis but gets significantly less than what the valuer had indicated. To protect themselves from a possible lawsuit, valuers make conservative estimates.

By clearly indicating that I would not be selling my property I eliminated that possible threat, giving the valuer a high degree of comfort.

To get the valuer into a generous and hopefully sympathetic frame of mind, I told him that the valuation was for bank purposes only, and was to help me settle a property I had recently purchased. A good valuation would enable me to obtain bank finance and settle my new property. Although this was not entirely true, I honestly had (and still have) no intention of selling my apartment. The higher valuation *was* intended to help me buy a new investment property—I just hadn't found it yet.

Summary

- Choose a property that's been sold within the past six months
- Get comparative sales results from real estate agents, from local newspapers and by checking the Valuer General's records
- Collate and review these sales results, then decide on a range that you'd be satisfied with in a valuation. Settle on a minimum, realistic maximum, and likely outcome
- Tell estate agents you're considering sell-

ing your property, and get their opinions of its sale and rental value
- Collect positive stories about the real estate market from the local press
- Use evidence and persuasion to get a higher valuation
- If possible, present the evidence in your favor before the valuer inspects the property
- Demonstrate that you know the property market in your area and don't have unrealistic expectations
- Say you're not planning to sell: this will prevent the valuer from trying to protect themselves by giving a conservative estimate

2. The Quantity Surveyor

Access that equity!

Having achieved my first goal of obtaining a suitable valuation and creating additional equity in my property, it was time to proceed to the next step—turning that equity into money and increasing my bank balance.

Having more equity in your property is like seeing the value of your shares increase. It gives you a feeling of wellbeing, but means little until you've sold your investment and taken the profit.

To access the new equity in my apartment, I decided to re-finance my existing home loan. But before approaching the bank, I wanted to put together a comprehensive report detailing my financial position.

Some readers may have personally refinanced a loan, or know someone who has. Although the effort I went to wasn't necessarily required to re-finance my property, I compiled a financial report because I would use this information again when I applied for new investment home loans.

What's a quantity surveyor?

My next step was to obtain a quantity surveyor's report. I use a quantity surveyor to find every legally depreciable item in my property, and then provide a schedule of those items showing straight-line depreciation and reducing-balance depreciation, and the economic lifespan of each item.

Examples of depreciation schedules can be obtained from most new large residential property developments. Depreciation schedules are usually provided to prospective investors to show the tax deductions claimable at the end of the financial year. Depreciation schedules are particularly prevalent when purchasers have the option to buy a furniture package with the property.

For readers who have never seen a quantity surveyor's report, I recommend that you visit the display suite of a large residential development and request a copy of the depreciation schedule. Here are some of the items included in a quantity surveyor's report.

- building
- floor coverings
- light fittings
- electrical appliances
- window furnishings
- air-conditioning units
- ducted vacuum units
- automated garage door control unit
- heating systems
- alarm systems
- hot water system

Remember that tax legislation differs between countries and jurisdictions. It frequently changes, and those items mentioned above may not always remain depreciable under the tax laws that apply to you and your properties.

Why you want a quantity surveyor's report

I obtain a quantity surveyor's report for a number of reasons.

The first is that naturally I want to claim the maximum depreciation allowable in my tax return. To make sure that I don't overlook anything, and that the information I provide to my accountant is true and correct, I use a professional quantity surveyor.

The second reason is simply convenience. As I mentioned above, tax legislation frequently changes and I don't have the knowledge or inclination to keep abreast of it. Probably, neither do you. I freely admit it is not my area of expertise. For a nominal fee, a quantity surveyor can save you far more in tax than what they charge, and the cost incurred is tax deductible.

The third reason for obtaining a depreciation schedule now, rather than waiting until the end of the financial year, was that I wanted to include this information in a comprehensive financial report for the bank.

When I approach the banks for loans I want to be treated like a professional investor, and when making any decisions regarding an investment you must know, in advance, every financial consideration relating to your investment. Banks who give you loans are investing in your knowledge of the investment, as much as, in the investment itself. They want every pertinent detail relating to the security of their money and your ability to service the loan.

Any investment property that I buy must be self-sufficient. The income generated by rent, and taking into account any tax benefits such as depreciation, must cover all expenses incurred by the property. These expenses include loan repayments, rates, and body corporate fees.

By giving the information from the depreciation schedule in my financial report, I wanted to show that an increased loan secured against my existing property would be fully funded by income from that existing property. Also, a depreciation schedule from a professional quantity surveyor lent credibility to my report, because the quantity surveyor is independent and has no vested interest in my property.

Summary

- After getting a good valuation on your property, you'll want to access your new equity
- A quantity surveyor's report is a good addition to the financial reports you'll give to the bank when refinancing or applying for a new loan
- Quantity surveyors give you an independent opinion on all the items in your property that are depreciable
- Having a quantity surveyor's depreciation schedule can save you money on taxes, and also saves you the trouble of keeping up with tax regulations yourself.

3. The Financial Analysis

Get a DIY financial analysis package

Not only has our society's interest in investing and making money led to an increase in the number of investment seminars, it has also spawned a large variety of money magazines. As well as running articles about making money, they also show ads promoting do-it-yourself financial analysis packages.

These DIY packages are fantastic. Of course, I haven't tried every package available, but those I have seen are easy to use and can instantaneously tell you how an investment property is geared. Negatively geared properties cost you more money than they make from rent. Neutrally geared properties cover the costs associated with keeping them through rental income. And positively geared properties leave you with money over after all costs have been accounted for. This last scenario is the most desirable scenario.

Some of the information required to generate an accurate analysis includes:

- Property price (what you paid for it)
- Property value (what you'd get if you sold it now)
- Outlays (costs incurred purchasing the property, such as taxes and legal fees)
- Loan details (outstanding borrowings and interest rate)
- Rent (allowances can be made for possible vacancy)
- Outgoings (all costs of holding the property, other than loan repayments, such as council rates and maintenance)
- Capital growth (estimated figure only)
- Inflation rate (estimated figure only)
- Depreciation (information from quantity surveyor's report)
- Personal income (for tax purposes)

This may seem like a fairly extensive list, but by obtaining an independent valuation, estate agents' rental estimates, and a quantity surveyor's report, I had all the information I needed to complete a financial analysis of the property.

As I mentioned earlier, in my case the property *price* I paid for my apartment was $205,000, and the property *value* had been independently assessed as $245,000. My *outlays* consisted of stamp duty and conveyancing costs.

All the information you'll need

Loan details relate to the amount of money you wish to borrow against the security of the property, and the interest rate the lender will charge you. At this stage you can choose between interest-only or principal and interest repayments, and you can see how this choice alone can significantly impact on how your property is geared and your ability to service the loan. Current interest rates can be found in any large daily newspaper, by searching the Internet or by calling any bank/lending institution. To determine **rent** I used the average of the three rental estimates I had obtained.

Outgoings I knew from having lived in my apartment for six months. In the case of a new property, I recommend you use the outgoings amount shown in the vendor's statement section 32, which accompanies any contract of sale. If your property is in another state or country, you might need to look elsewhere for this information. This figure, whilst only being an estimate, must not be less than what the actual outgoings will be once the property settles. As a result, in my experience, this figure is always generous.

Capital growth of the property into the future will always be nothing more than a guess. In my analysis I used a conservative 7 percent annual growth estimate. The reason I believe this is conservative is because although annual capital growth rates will fluctuate over a 10-year period, the general consensus is that a property's value should double after this time, and from past sales evidence the capital growth around my property (in this case the CBD) had easily exceeded 10 percent per annum on average over the previous ten years.

The **inflation rate**, like the capital growth rate, over an extended period is nothing more than an estimate. In my analysis I used a rate one percentage point higher than the inflation rate at the time.

The figures I used for **depreciation** (there are separate depreciation amounts for building and for fittings and fixtures) were provided by the quantity surveyor.

Finally, there was **personal income**, which in my case wasn't immediately clear. Because I had decided to leave my recent employment, I was without a regular weekly income. During the period I was preparing my financial report, I occasionally worked on a casual basis. As part of my report I included a letter from an employer stating that I was working as a contractor on a set daily rate, which also showed a projected figure over a 12-month period. I did this to give the impression that I was earning a regular salary, and to avoid the necessity of providing old tax returns and group certificates.

Prepare for the worst

The benefit of using a DIY software package is that the financial analysis will immediately calculate how your property is geared before and after tax. By manipulating the numbers you can see the minimum rent you must achieve to have a positively geared investment. Your inputs can be changed to see in advance what affect a changing market may have on your property and ultimately your hip pocket.

When doing such an analysis, you can be as conservative or optimistic as you like. In fact, you can try both outlooks in turn. You can project how the equity in your property will grow in the future, and you can change your loan type from interest-only to principal and interest, enabling you to determine your best financial strategy. You can even change your annual salary to take into account any promotions you hope to secure, and you can see how salary increases (and the different tax brackets) affect your personal tax position in relation to how well geared your property is.

Using all the information I had gathered, I determined that I could easily positively gear my apartment based on a rental figure much lower than the estimates provided by the estate agents.

Because of my conservative nature I produced a financial analysis showing conservative estimates in all the input fields. My report showed loan interest rates, outgoings and inflation rates much higher than necessary, and taxable income and rental lower than indicated in my accompanying documentation.

Importantly, though, I never took my eye off the bottom line—I wanted to ensure my property was positively geared. I prepared my financial analysis using these conservative inputs because as an investor you must be prepared for the worst-case scenario, and I needed to show the bank that this was so.

Summary

- Get a DIY financial analysis package
- Collect the information you need, and input it to see whether your property is positively, negatively, or neutrally geared
- Experiment with different parameters in your analysis to see how different scenarios could play out
- In your final analysis, be conservative so the bank can see you're prepared for the worst

4. The Personal Balance Sheet

Establishing that I could positively gear my apartment was a crucial step. Had I not been satisfied my property would make a good investment, the alternative would have been to sell the apartment and purchase another more suitable investment property.

My next step was to prepare a personal balance sheet. As the name suggests, it was a simple table showing my personal assets and liabilities, as well as my monthly income and expenses. Primarily, I put this information together because I knew the bank would require it before considering any loan application. The table I used was simple in style and content, but comprehensive in its list of inclusions.

Because I was not starting my new venture from a position of substantial financial strength, I wanted to make this document appear as impressive and comprehensive as possible. The reason for making each section of my financial report as informative as possible was to anticipate every personal and financial detail that the lending institution might reasonably require when determining my eligibility for a loan.

More importantly, by including this information up-front I wanted the lender to accept my financial report, with all its inclusions and conclusions, as true and correct.

To make my personal balance sheet appear more impressive, I included such items as superannuation, even though I had no intention of using these funds to help me build a property portfolio.

I also included a figure for household furniture and my car. Some insurance companies offer agreed value policies for things like furniture and cars, that allow you to determine (within reason) their replacement value if they are stolen or damaged. The extra cost of such a policy is often minimal. For readers like me, who are starting with a relatively small asset base, I recommend increasing the level of your car and furniture insurance. In my case, the cost was nominal, so I increased my cover to a much higher value.

Because banks and the like do not inspect cars and furnishings, they will generally accept your stated value. If your stated value is the same as the insured value it adds credibility to your personal balance sheet.

Because lenders anticipate that borrowers will inflate the value of their car(s) and furnishings, they will often only take these items into consideration at a much lower figure than you have indicated. They may even dismiss these items entirely when assessing a loan application. Despite this, I recommend that you include as much as possible in the asset column of your personal balance sheet. While initially, your loan application may be assessed by a computer, ultimately you are writing for a person who can start you on the road to owning your first investment property.

Many people with a steady income do not have a large amount of money saved, and may not have a share portfolio. If you do not have a history of saving or servicing a loan, personal items such as cars and furnishings may be taken into consideration. These could make the difference between securing an investment loan or not. Without furnishings you will appear to be a spendthrift, and the loan assessor will be hesitant to approve your loan.

I also included a monthly salary and rental figures. As mentioned earlier, I had a letter from an employer stating that I was working as a contractor. Included in that letter was a projected income figure over a twelve-month period. To calculate my monthly salary I simply divided this figure by twelve.

Personal balance sheet

Assets		Liabilities	
Investment property	$245,000	Home loan	$192,000
Car	$30,000	Visa card	$5,000
Home furnishings	$40,000		
Superannuation	$55,000		
Savings account	$5,000		
Total	$375,000	**Total**	$197,000

Incoming/month		Outgoing/month	
Salary	$3,200	Home loan payments	$1,062
Rental	$1,581	Visa card	$1,500
Total	$4,781	**Total**	$2,562

To determine rent, I took the average of the three rental estimates I had obtained. I included a projected rental figure, even though my property was not being rented, because I wanted to show that the anticipated monthly rental exceeded my monthly loan repayments. With the projected rent, the total incoming easily exceeded my outgoing figure. Naturally, if the property were let, I would include the actual rental figure.

Summary

- Create a personal balance sheet to demonstrate your eligibility for a loan
- Include *all* your assets on the balance sheet, including things like home furnishings, your car, and superannuation
- Also include your liabilities, and your monthly incomings and outgoings
- Consider taking out insurance to protect your assets and so you can use your insurance statement to demonstrate their value
- If you have a rental property that's not currently let, use an estimate of projected rental income in your list of monthly incomings

5. The Individual Credit Report

An individual credit report contains information that will assist subscribers in making credit decisions. Subscribers include banks and lending institutions, along with a wide range of other services.

An individual credit report includes personal details such as:

- current residential address
- driver's licence
- employment details
- bankruptcy information
- overdue accounts
- loan applications

Anyone can have a copy of their own individual credit report. The bank has the same copy. Naturally, before a lending institution lets you borrow, they want to know your credit standing. Having an individual credit report lets you show the institution that you know your financial resources well.

I have always included a copy of my individual credit report in my financial report. I always received an overwhelmingly positive reaction to its inclusion. Usually, the loan assessors told me that they have never seen a copy of this report provided by the applicant. Many were amazed that I was even aware that this report exists.

I want to be viewed as a professional and knowledgeable investor. By including all pertinent information, I make my financial report more clearly true and correct.

Check for accuracy

A more practical and important reason for having a copy of your individual credit report is to check its accuracy.

On one occasion, I was preparing my financial report for an investment property I had purchased. I ordered my credit report and discovered an entry for a deposit bond of $2.85 million. The properties I bought totalled $2.85 million, but the deposit bond I had applied for was for only $180,000.

I called the company that issued the bond and received a letter explaining the error. I attached the letter to my credit report to prove to the lending institute that my credit report was incorrect.

The lending institute accepted this and I secured my investment loan and settled the property I had bought. Later, I forwarded a copy of the letter from the deposit bond company to the credit report issuer and had the error corrected.

Any comments or entries shown on your individual credit report cannot be removed, only changed, and only with the acknowledgment of the credit provider who is responsible for the error.

Finding an error in my credit report taught me a valuable lesson about being prepared. If I had not found this error I would not have raised the matter with the lending institution, and my application would probably have been rejected. Banks or lending institutions are not required to provide a reason for declining a loan application. If I had not discovered the credit report error, it may have led to multiple rejections and serious financial consequences.

Loan requirement

Your application for an investment home loan may be approved subject to a satisfactory credit report. This means that your application can be assessed based on the information provided in your financial report, but once the lending institute is prepared to approve your loan, they may request your credit report for a final check.

Usually when an application for a loan is made, the lending institution first checks your credit report. If this report is not satisfactory, say for instance you are bankrupt or have numerous unpaid accounts, your loan will be immediately rejected. This is a time-saving measure for the lending institution. There is no need to even consider a loan application if the applicant's credit report is unsatisfactory.

Avoid marks on your credit report

Every time a credit provider inquires, your credit report is marked. It's also marked if you make multiple loan applications, or if you have a loan rejected. Lending institutions do not look favourably on credit reports with lots of marks.

In order to maintain control of my credit report, I do not permit any inquiry until my loan application has been approved in principle. A credit provider is not allowed to view your individual credit report without your written consent. Although I include a copy of my individual credit report in my financial report, the lending institution will still insist on obtaining their own copy, just in case it's been marked since I obtained my copy. They also want to check that I have not unlawfully altered my copy.

Summary

- Get an individual credit report
- Make changes to your credit report if any details are incorrect
- Lending institutions use individual credit reports to check your credit standing
- Do not permit any credit check until loan application has been approved in principle

6. Comprehensive Insurance Cover

Having a home insurance policy is a must

Most people know what insurance is, including home insurance and contents insurance. In my opinion, both are essential for any homeowner.

When buying a home, it is generally recommended that you take out a home insurance policy as soon as you sign a contract of sale. Most conveyors I spoke with think that if you have signed a contract of sale for a property, as the buyer, you still have an insurable interest in that property—even before the property has settled.

Therefore, if there is inadequate building insurance cover, you may stand to lose, even if the property is damaged before settlement takes place.

One example given to me was a property that was damaged by fire after the sale had occurred, but before the settlement date. The vendors did not have insurance to cover the damage, and the buyers had not taken out a policy on the property.

The property was still livable, and settlement took place even though the property was damaged.

If a property is damaged prior to settlement, the vendor's insurance is used first to rectify the damage. The purchaser's insurance policy is applied as a secondary measure if the vendor's insurance is inadequate.

Why you need a landlord insurance policy

I already had home and contents insurance policies for my apartment. When planning to rent my apartment, I took out a landlord insurance policy as well, after researching numerous policies and companies. I believe landlord insurance is necessary for any investment property.

A landlord insurance policy covers things such as:

- damage caused to the property by the tenant
- lost rent due to damage caused by the tenant
- rent default due to a tenant breaking their lease
- legal expenses

I included details of my insurance in a simple table, listing the insurance provider and details of the level of cover provided. My table included details of the building and contents insurance I already had, as well as the landlord insurance I intended to take out once I rented my apartment.

The importance of personal insurance policies

The logic behind personal insurance policies is simple: if something unexpected happens to me, I do not want to leave my loved ones with a financial burden.

To feel as secure as possible, and also to give the lending institution peace of mind, I also took out insurance policies for:

- private health cover
- death cover
- income protection insurance
- total temporary disability
- total permanent disability

Researching these insurances was the last step to completing my financial report.

Although I love real estate and I enthusiastically talk about it with anyone who has a similar passion, I know some people consider investment properties cumbersome and troublesome.

Without insurance, if I die unexpectedly, my loved ones would have at least some financial security from the equity in my properties. However, with the appropriate insurance cover, my properties will pass to my heirs completely debt free, because the mortgages will be paid by my insurance policies.

Some readers may not be comfortable thinking about life insurance. Personally, I feel far more comfortable knowing that my loved ones will inherit debt-free real estate in the event that I die unexpectedly. Rather than receiving rent to service the mortgage and rely upon capital growth to make money, the rent becomes a regular and significant passive income. Any capital growth is considered a bonus.

How comprehensive insurance policies help

Comprehensive insurance is primarily for my benefit, but it also provides security for lending institutions. Each time I purchase a new property, I increase the level of my insurance policies to cover the additional debt. If I die or become permanently disabled, all my debt is covered. If I become temporarily disabled, incapacitated, or unable to work, I have appropriate insurance cover.

I showed in my financial report that my investment property was independently valued and worth more than the loan. This is like insurance for the bank. If I cannot meet my mortgage obligations, the bank or lending institution can foreclose the mortgage, secure the property, and subsequently sell the property and recover their money.

By providing details of the independent valuation and my insurance policies, I am showing the banks that I have thought of every conceivable accident to the property and to myself. In doing so, I am showing them that their money is absolutely safe when loaned to me. Remember, I do this so that the banks and lending institutions consider me as a professional investor.

An example of the table I provide in my financial report showing all the insurances I have is shown on page 57.

I do not include a copy of the actual insurance policies in my financial report because I feel it would be excessive. A brief description of the level of cover provided by each policy is sufficient to demonstrate my thoroughness, and most financiers I have spoken with know what the different insurances are. Indeed, most lenders are able to offer their clients most of these insurance policies.

Another good source for these insurances was my superannuation providers. I found they were inexpensive compared to their competitors, and the premiums were paid direct from my superannuation funds.

Summary

- Get a home insurance policy as soon as you sign a contract of sale, to cover accidental damages before settlement
- Get a contents insurance policy
- Get a landlord insurance policy if you plan to rent your property
- Get other personal insurance policies to cover unexpected death and disability to secure the future of your loved ones
- Personal insurance policies guarantee security to banks and lending institutions

Personal insurances

Type	Insurer / Amount / Policy No.
Private health	Health fund name Type of hospital cover – membership no.
Income protection	Insurance company name Level of income protection – member no.
Total permanent disability (TPD)	Insurance company name Level of cover – policy no.
Total temporary disability (TTD)	Insurance company name Level of cover – policy no.
Death cover	Insurance company name Level of cover – policy no.

Property insurances

Type	Insurer / Amount / Policy No.
Building	Insurance company name Level of cover – policy no.
Contents insurance	Insurance company name Level of cover – policy no.
Rental (landlord insurance)	Insurance company name Level of cover – policy no.

7. The Financial Report

My financial report brought together all the information I had collected.

The contents page read as follows:

1. Personal balance sheet
2. Detailed financial analysis
3. Copy of independent bank valuation
4. Copy of quantity surveyor's report
5. Twelve-month rental estimates
6. Salary confirmation
7. Individual credit report
8. Comprehensive insurance cover
9. Evidence of comparable sales

Securing your loan by providing a financial report

I hope this comprehensive document will be the key to securing an unlimited number of investment home loans, which will lead to my becoming a millionaire. In the immediate future, I hope it will enable me to refinance my existing home loan.

The report comprised hundreds of pages, and I doubt that anyone other than myself has read its entire contents. Nevertheless, the size of the document gave the impression that I had prepared it thoroughly, as indeed I had.

I included all the information listed above because I want the lending institutions to accept my financial report and all its reports, letters, inclusions and conclusions as true and correct.

Why rental estimates help

Item 5 in my financial report is the twelve-month rental estimates. Initially, I obtained these estimates for the benefit of the valuer, prior to obtaining an independent valuation of my apartment. Later, I used the average of the three rental estimates to complete my financial analysis and help me determine whether my investment would be positively, negatively or neutrally geared.

I included the rental estimates in my financial report to support my financial analysis, and to show that my rental figure was not an over-inflated fabrication, but a reasonable expectation based on information provided by local estate agents.

Provide comparable sales evidence

Item 9, the comparable sales evidence, was also collected primarily for the benefit of the valuer. I included this information because it shows similar properties to mine that sold for far more than my property.

Banks are only interested in the valuer's opinion, but including my own sales evidence supports the generally accepted view that valuers are usually conservative in their estimates.

Choosing valuation firms

Banks expect valuers to be conservative and will not dismiss the valuer's estimation. By including comparable sales, I am providing further evidence that the bank's money is safe. If my loan application hangs in the balance, this additional information may be the added security the bank needs to approve my loan.

Another reason for including my comparable sales evidence is that although I obtain my independent valuations from a firm approved by the bank, the bank may still insist on obtaining their own valuation.

Banks may do this because the bank's list of preferred valuers is usually broken up into smaller lists, recommending particular firms for particular geographical areas. Therefore, the valuation firm I use may not be the bank's preferred firm for the area in which I have purchased my investment property.

Of course, there are far too many valuation firms and valuers to get to know them all. When I choose a valuation firm, I base my decision on which firms appear on the panel of all the major banks. The firm I use is a large, reputable, well-known company. Within this firm I use a particular valuer.

Through numerous dealings I have developed a rapport with my preferred valuer, and by demonstrating my knowledge of the real estate market I am able to obtain satisfactory independent valuations. To maintain this relationship I use the same valuer regardless of the property's location.

When the bank chooses another valuer

Sometimes my preferred valuer is not the bank's first preference for that particular area. In these instances the bank sends a copy of my independent valuation, and my comparable sales evidence, to their preferred firm, and requests a new valuation. The new valuation figure has always concurred with my figure.

The most likely reason for this is that valuations are subjective. Unless the second valuer strongly disagrees with my independent valuation figure, and is able to support his or her own opinion, he or she will simply concur with the first valuer's estimate to avoid dispute. A second valuer is more likely to concur if the first estimate came from a large, reputable firm.

A valuation can, however, be disputed. If relevant information was not taken into consideration, the valuation can be changed. Remember that a sworn valuer can be sued for negligence.

If a valuer is presented with another recent valuation from a respected firm, together with supporting documentation and sales evidence, the path of least resistance is usually taken.

Finally, when a bank requests a new valuation, I always comply, but I refuse to pay for the second valuation. After all, I have already incurred costs by using an approved valuer from their panel. The banks I used have always agreed to meet the cost of a second valuation, if they required one to satisfy their internal policies.

Summary

- Make a comprehensive financial report
- A detailed financial report increases your chances
- Include comparable sales in your financial report
- Choose your own valuer and develop a good relationship with them
- Have the bank pay if they require a second valuation

8. Securing a Loan

Armed with my financial report, I decided it was now time to see my bank about refinancing my existing home loan. I wanted to enter into a new mortgage agreement, based upon the independent valuation I had obtained.

When I purchased my apartment, the amount of the loan was calculated as a percentage of the contract price, which was $205,000. If I was able to secure a new loan on the same terms, but the independent valuation of $245,000 was used in lieu of the contract price, I stood to receive approximately $30,000.

This money was crucial to enable me to start my new venture, but I also needed it to live, as I no longer had a regular weekly income.

Failure is not fatal

I contacted my bank and made an appointment to see the lending manager. After a fairly anticlimactic meeting, I was told that my loan application had been declined.

The ensuing duel with the lending manager was not as successful, or as satisfying, as when I fought for an independent valuation for my apartment. For one thing, my negotiation with the valuer had been in person, whereas, on the phone, the lending manager could simply hang up on me—and, at one point, he did.

However, I was informed that although the bank had rejected my loan, they might reconsider my application and approve the loan if I used it to pay a deposit on a new investment property.

This did leave me the opportunity to continue negotiations, and, perhaps, achieve my aim of a refinanced loan. But, whether due to my conservative nature or to my general mistrust toward banks, I was not tempted. Even after I'd found an investment property to purchase, the bank only might refinance my existing loan. They might not.

Of course, my other concern was that my savings were being rapidly depleted. I needed a much more favourable outcome, and fast.

Don't fail to try again

My next step was to approach another bank.

Just as I did when I invited a second valuer to inspect my apartment, I reviewed my approach for the upcoming meeting with the new bank. I re-assessed my financial report and rehearsed what to say, summarising each section of the report. I practised doing this while the report was open and facing away from me, just as it would be when I was sitting opposite a lending manager.

A few days later I met with the lending manager at a different bank, one that I had never dealt with before. Because they knew nothing about me or my financial position, I spent more time with this manager as I went through each section of my report.

I paid particular attention to the financial analysis and emphasised that the property would be a positively geared investment once it was rented at the conservative rental estimate shown in my report. Unlike with the first bank, I left the meeting confident.

The next day I was told that my new loan was approved, and the additional funds of about $30,000 would be deposited into my nominated account.

The trials I went through refinancing my existing home loan may not happen to everyone. Many people will be in a more financially secure position than I was when I started. Some may have already refinanced an existing loan.

For me, this journey was not just about one loan for one property. It was about discovering every hurdle I would need to overcome to reach my goal of acquiring unlimited positively geared, or at least neutrally geared, investment properties.

Unfortunately, my initial excitement did not last long after receiving the additional funds. My next task was to remove all personal debts with the money I had obtained from re-financing my home loan.

Good debt, bad debt

I paid off my credit card debts, which were accumulating debt and interest at an alarming rate, due to my hiatus from full-time work. I also paid an outstanding car loan. The interest charged on these two forms of credit was considerably higher than the interest charged on my home loan.

I also wanted to remove all personal debts because, unlike business or investment loans, personal loans have no tax benefits. Interest paid on personal debts cannot be claimed, while interest on business loans or investment loans can be.

All accountants enthusiastically advise reducing personal debt. Many books deal specifically with this matter. One such book I have read, and that I recommend, is *Rich Dad, Poor Dad*, by Robert Kiyosaki. This book describes in plain language the difference between good debt and bad debt.

Put simply, a bad debt must be paid by you and has no tax benefits. A good debt has tax benefits and is paid on your behalf by another party.

One example of bad debt that most people can relate to is credit card interest. Most cards provide you with a line of credit of up to 45 days. If you pay your credit card bill in full each month, without incurring any interest costs, credit cards can be a great convenience. However, if you do not pay your credit card in full each month, then penalty interest is charged and you may become buried in debt. This is bad debt because no one will pay the debt on your behalf and the interest charged cannot be claimed as a tax deduction.

A common example of good debt is an investment home loan. Tenants pay rent, which can be used to pay interest on the loan. If the rent is not enough to pay the interest on the loan in full, the extra cost can be claimed in your tax return and will reduce your taxable income. This is commonly referred to as negative gearing.

Tax legislation varies from state to state. Seek independent financial advice about what can and cannot be claimed for tax purposes.

After removing my bad debt, it was time to find a tenant for my apartment.

Summary

- Refinance your existing home loan
- Seek another bank if the first one rejects your loan application
- Remove all personal debts once your loan application is approved
- A good debt is paid on your behalf by another party and has tax benefits
- A bad debt has no tax benefits and is paid by you alone

9. Renting

I obtained three rental estimates from local estate agents. But I invited only two of those agents back to lease my property.

As a personal preference, I always appoint only two real estate agencies when leasing any of my investment properties.

I believe there is sufficient competition between two agencies to ensure that I get the best rental result possible. It's also easy to stay in contact with them and keep abreast of progress.

Furnished or unfurnished?

To get the highest possible rent, I decided to lease my apartment furnished. Although my furnishings were inexpensive, they complemented the apartment and greatly added to the property's appeal. My furniture was also new, so I could depreciate it fully at tax time. To attract as many people as possible, I listed my apartment with and without furniture at both my chosen agents.

The unfurnished rental figure was much higher than the agents recommended, and the furnished rental figure was considerably lower. By doing this, whether the apartment was leased furnished or unfurnished, the rent would easily cover my loan repayments and other costs relating to the property.

Be personal

My experience as an estate agent gave me the confidence to deal with people. When agents wanted to show prospective tenants through my apartment, I conducted the inspection. This will not be feasible for all, but I believe the best way to maximise your rent is to show prospective tenants through your property personally.

No estate agent can know your property as well as you do. They will never be as enthusiastic as you, as you have more to gain. I had lived in my apartment for the past six months. I had also only recently purchased the furniture, so I could confirm that everything was new and working perfectly.

Another benefit of conducting inspections personally is that you can choose your tenant.

I found a tenant for my apartment within the first week of listing the property. I was able to negotiate a twelve-month lease with furniture. And because I agreed to buy a new washing machine for the tenant's use, I was able to secure a higher rent than I'd advertised.

Everybody wins

Because the tenant was referred to my property by an estate agent, and to ensure I kept a good relationship with the agent, I still paid the full letting fee and management fee. After I negotiated the lease, I sent my new tenant to the agent's office to sign the necessary documentation, and the agent carried out the normal tenant checks.

At all times I endeavour to keep dealings between the agents, tenants and myself fair and reasonable. After all, if each party believes that they have won from the transaction, future negotiations will be easier and more harmonious.

By negotiating the lease directly with the tenants, the estate agent won because I did the inspection and most of the work for them, but I still paid the full fees to the agency.

The tenants won because although the rent is high for a seventy square metre, two-bedroom apartment, it is cheap for a furnished apartment. Undoubtedly this was mainly why the tenants renewed their lease after twelve months, but I believe another contributing factor was the rapport we struck when we initially negotiated the lease.

And of course, I won. My property was positively geared, and the tenants continued to rent it beyond the initial lease period.

By getting to know the tenants, I could inspect my property on short notice when necessary and they could contact me directly if any major problems arose.

A passive income

According to my financial analysis, the rent was enough to ensure that my investment is positively geared. Even after expenses such as council rates, interest on the loan, body corporate fees, and insurance, the property made me an extra $5,000. This was before considering depreciation for tax purposes after the first twelve months.

This was my first foray into developing a property portfolio. I still use it as a model for all my investments. The apartment has been positively geared from the beginning, and the equity I have in the property enabled me to buy additional properties—exactly the result I hoped for.

I know the rent I receive will cover all expenses, and I even have some money left to enjoy life or for any unforeseen emergencies.

If any of my tenants agree to renew their lease, I do not increase the rent. Because I fix the interest rate on my investment home loans, I know that my outgoings remain the same from year to year, unaffected by inflation. I am certain how my investment will be geared at the beginning of each financial year.

By ensuring that each investment property is at least neutrally geared, I can sit back and let the investment grow in value without the stress or the need to contribute any of my own money to pay expenses.

Why do I rent?

Having secured a tenant for my apartment, I now needed to find a home to live in. I decided to rent, for a number of reasons.

Renting a home is much cheaper than buying a home and paying off a mortgage. This may appear to be a peculiar thing to say, now that I own several properties. But there are important differences between renting and buying.

As a tenant, you naturally pay rent, but you do

not pay for maintenance of the property, council rates, body corporate fees, or water. For the homeowner, on the other hand, these extra expenses can amount to thousands of dollars.

Most importantly, a landlord can claim all out of pocket expenses at tax time. A homeowner receives no tax concessions.

It is still possible to find properties—and not dumps—where the rent is far less than the mortgage repayments would be.

As a general rule, cheaper homes tend to attract better rent returns than more expensive homes. When I was selling real estate in the outer suburbs of Melbourne, a three-bedroom home worth $150,000 would typically rent for about $220 per week, giving the owner a return of approximately 7.6 percent. By contrast, a home worth $400,000 would usually rent for about $400 per week, providing a return of about 5.2 percent.

This is still the case. While the figures may be higher in today's market as a rule the more expensive the home is, the lower the rental return it will achieve, when expressed as a percentage.

Percentage returns are based on a 52-week rent and do not include expenses such as council rates or water.

More expensive homes usually receive lower rental returns because there are fewer prospective tenants who can afford higher rents. Expensive homes can often remain vacant for extended periods, waiting for the right tenant.

In my experience, though, this is not of great concern for the owners of these expensive homes. If the owner can afford to hold onto the property, even at a lower rent, the property will have grown more in value than most cheaper-priced homes, and the owner will receive a larger capital gain.

Though I did not live in a dump, I certainly could not afford a mansion. But by taking my time searching the rental market, I could find a good home at a reasonable rent.

Something to keep in mind when choosing a property to rent is that trendy suburbs attract the highest rent. If you live in a suburb next to a fashionable one, you can still have the convenience of living near cafés and restaurants, while saving substantially on your weekly rent.

Regardless of where you look, you can usually find perfectly good homes that have been listed for rent for some time. These homes can often be leased for less than the advertised amount.

Why people think otherwise

Renting does not appeal to all. Many people dream of buying the perfect home and paying it off. Although this dream is a very common one, it may not make economic sense.

The most common reasons people give for wanting to buy a home to live in are:

- Renting is too expensive
- Rent money is wasted money
- A home is a good investment
- The security of living in your own home and not being evicted
- Capital growth
- Paying off your home loan is a good form of saving

Is it really that expensive?

Renting is not necessarily expensive. Many people rent because some homes are simply too expensive to buy. Remember, tenants do not have to pay expenses relating to the property.

The money you save towards buying a home could be used to pay rent on a better home. While you may not be able to buy a million-dollar mansion, a lot of people may be able to live in one, if only they would consider renting.

The phrase "rent money is wasted money" is a common expression many of us would remember hearing from our parents. But paying interest on a mortgage to a bank is also wasted money.

Investing in a home

"A home is a good investment" is another familiar statement. This is undoubtedly true in most cases. But I wonder how many people would have bought the home they live in, had they been buying solely as an investment.

As an estate agent, I always preferred selling a home to an owner-occupier than an investor. Someone buying a home to live in is far more emotionally attached to a home than the analytical, discerning investor. Negotiating with the dreamy-eyed would-be homeowner is far easier, and they are far more likely to pay more to secure the property.

Owner-occupiers buy a home to suit their own requirements. On the other hand, I believe an investor should consider the tenants' requirements when selecting properties.

For example, younger tenants will often rent with a friend, making rent more affordable. In such cases, each tenant's only private area is their bedroom. For this reason, tenants often prefer large bedrooms to large living areas.

For similar reasons, I believe it is advantageous to have two bathrooms in an investment property. That way tenants do not have to clean up after themselves immediately. They can leave their clothes and personal toiletries lying around.

Another difference between the home buyer and the investor is that the home buyer will purchase wherever they can afford to. They are not necessarily looking for areas with the greatest capital growth. Home buyers are primarily looking for a property which suits their requirements, and will look in areas where they can afford such a property.

In contrast, an investor's first goal is to identify those areas that achieve maximum capital growth and to buy well-priced properties in those areas. Although homes in these areas may be more expensive, rents should also be higher.

Security

Peace of mind, in the belief that you cannot be evicted, is another reason often given for purchasing a property to live in.

Tenants' rights have become more powerfully protected with each new draft of the Landlord and Tenant Act. Some landlords believe tenants have too many rights, but I believe the protection given to tenants is necessary and fair.

Once a tenant enters into a lease, that tenant deserves the right to enjoy their tenancy unless the agreement is breached. Current legislation states that unless there are extraordinary circumstances, a tenant cannot be evicted from the home they are renting. The only way a landlord can evict a tenant prior to the expiration of a lease is to apply for a hearing before a tribunal and apply for a reduced term of lease due to personal hardship such as bankruptcy.

Before this legislation was introduced, landlords often broke leases. This frequently happened when the landlord wanted to sell their property. A landlord could serve the tenant with a 60-day notice to vacate, enabling the property to be sold as vacant. Under the current legislation, this can no longer happen.

Legislation varies greatly from state to state and often changes. It is advisable to speak with a qualified property manager in your area.

Renting can be more secure than you think...

Increasingly, residential properties are rented for longer leases with the right of renewal. These leases are common with commercial properties. They work just like a normal lease, with a fixed term and fixed rent, but instead of the typical six-month or twelve-month lease, longer leases can run for up to five years or more.

Usually, these leases have built-in rent increases. These increases are either by a nominated percentage each year, or are reviewed each year and may only increase with inflation.

The right to renew the lease is an option available exclusively to the tenant currently renting the property. It allows the tenant to renew the lease under the same terms and conditions as the old lease, to the exclusion of any other party. If the current tenant does not wish to exercise their right to renew under the same terms and conditions as the old lease, they may negotiate a new lease on new terms.

This type of lease is particularly popular with families who have children attending school. The longer lease provides stability. If desired, the child can complete their entire primary or secondary education at the same school.

It is also a popular option among businesses

who frequently relocate executives and want good quality housing. Rather than searching for rental properties each time staff relocate, businesses can secure long-term leases and know that their accommodation requirements are taken care of. The advantages of such leases for security and stability are clear. Businesses have been using these leases for commercial properties for decades.

If a five-year lease does not seem long enough, consider the average length of time that people live in a home they buy. Many buyers believe they will always live there, but in fact the average length of time living in a purchased home is only seven years.

Another advantage of this type of long term, renewable lease is that although they are still relatively new, such leases are a growing trend in residential real estate. If you approach a landlord and propose such a lease, it will generally be easier to negotiate a cheaper rent.

These leases are also advantageous for the landlord because they have secured a long-term tenant. They eliminate any concerns about the investment property being vacant for extended periods. They also eliminate the cost of advertising the property each year, when a traditional twelve-month lease expires.

... and owning a home can be less secure

Many homeowners may not be aware that most mortgage agreements allow the lender to change the terms of the mortgage agreement at any time without requiring the borrower's consent.

The lender may also waive their rights under the agreement, or at any time assign or transfer all or any part of their rights or obligations under the agreement. In fact, some mortgage agreements include a provision that allows the lender to call upon the funds provided under the mortgage agreement at any time.

If the lender calls upon the funds and the buyer is not able to repay the mortgage within the time frame requested, the lender may foreclose the loan and sell the home to retrieve their money. Although I doubt many lenders would do this due to the very bad press such behaviour would attract, their legal right to do so still shatters the illusion most home owners have that their home is untouchable.

After reading a typical mortgage agreement, and then reading the rights protecting tenants, many readers might be surprised to find that tenants enjoy more security of tenure than the average homeowner.

Real estate for capital growth

Capital growth is another reason for buying a home. In fact, it is the only reason I buy real estate. But I doubt many people would have bought their current home if capital growth were the only consideration. Capital growth comes from investment properties too, and investment properties grow in value just as much as owner-occupied homes.

Some people believe that a home will attract greater capital growth if the mortgage is paid off faster. This is not true.

As you reduce your mortgage, equity in your property will increase accordingly—as long as the value of your property has not decreased—but this has nothing to do with capital growth.

Most home loans, whether for investment or for owner-occupancy, are repaid on the basis of principal and interest. However many sacrifices you make, and however tirelessly you devote yourself to paying off your loan quickly, your home will not grow in value any more, or any faster.

Capital growth is a fantastic reason to invest in real estate, but it does not mean you have to buy a home to live in.

To rent or not to rent

Paying off a home is often said to be a good form of saving.

Over the years, I have seen many televised debates about the merits of renting a home versus buying a home to live in. On each occasion, the side in favour of renting has won, but not without some controversy. Both sides base their hypotheses on a number of variables and on many assumptions about those variables.

For instance, the argument in favour of renting assumes that the money tenants save by renting accumulates every week without exception, and that money is put into an interest-bearing savings account, unlike home owners paying off a mortgage.

Another argument in favour of renting assumes that repairs and maintenance, such as painting or new carpets, will be paid for by the homeowner and not by tenants.

The anti-renting argument assumes that tenants don't own investment properties, missing out on capital growth, and that tenants are subject to rent increases.

As I've shown, none of these things are necessarily true.

Paying off a mortgage on a home you live in is

a form of saving. But in my opinion, a better way to save is to minimise your expenses and invest any surplus income. One way of minimising your expenses is to rent a home rather than pay off a mortgage on a home you live in. This plan may not appeal to all readers, but I would prefer a savings plan that I am in control of. A mortgage is a savings plan dictated by the banks.

Renting has other advantages too. You can live in and experience different areas, and different types of homes. When a rental property gets old, you can simply pack your bags and look for something newer or newly renovated. A tenant doesn't have to worry about maintenance and renovations, which can cost the homeowner tens of thousands of dollars.

Renting offers tenants freedom and choices that are not easily enjoyed by homeowners who are servicing a mortgage.

Summary

- To reach a bigger market when renting your property, offer both furnished and unfurnished options for tenants
- Conduct inspections with your prospective tenants personally
- Have a good relationship with your agent and tenant to ensure good business with them
- A positively-geared investment guarantees stable income
- Renting is cheaper
- The law protects tenants' rights, whereas mortgaged homes can be repossessed
- Capital growth does not mean you have to buy a home to live in
- Renting offers more choices for the tenant

10. Searching for a New Investment

Now that my apartment was rented, I had a home to live in, I had more money in my bank account, and I had no more personal debts. I was ready to start searching for a new investment property.

Clearly, I was more appealing to the banks than when I first applied for a home loan. My new home and my investment loan were being fully paid for by my tenants, and there was money left over for me. My weekly expenses had decreased because the property I was renting was cheaper than the mortgage repayments I was making when I lived in my apartment. All these achievements substantially increased my borrowing capacity.

A homeowner only has his or her own income to rely on to service the debt, while an investor has two: the rent, plus his or her personal income. Because of this, investors are more likely than homeowners to service a mortgage.

My eagerness to expand my property portfolio was not only due to my new financial position. I was also stronger psychologically.

I am naturally conservative and was somewhat nervous about committing myself to too much debt. I had to overcome my self-doubts in order to achieve my goal. In preparing my financial report and negotiating with valuers, estate agents, and bank managers, I proved to myself that I could bring about my desired outcome, even if it meant overcoming some obstacles.

This psychological advance may seem trivial to readers who are financially better off, or more confident than I was. But for the nervous who want to test the water first, I recommend you take your time and carry out extensive research until you are absolutely convinced you can achieve your goals. I needed to go through a process of trial and error before taking the next step.

The extra money in my bank account helped convince me that I could earn more.

Looking for suburbs

Next, I needed to identify the suburbs that I wanted to invest in. I have read a lot of articles about the next real estate "hot spots"—the new areas that are predicted to boom. These articles may be accurate, but I decided to ignore them. Instead, I would select areas that were already considered upmarket. I chose blue-chip suburbs because I think they have always been viewed as expensive, desirable areas.

By the time you hear that a certain area is an investment "hot spot", most of the growth has already taken place without you. And even if these areas do grow enormously over the few years after you invest in them, the excitement—and the investment—often wane over the following ten years. There will always be a new "hot spot". Trends come and go.

Initially you may be happy with your purchase in a newly fashionable area, but in the long run, those areas that have always been popular and which experience steady, reliable growth will be a better investment.

Be careful of areas that are trendy because they are new

New areas may not yet even have facilities like supermarkets, schools, parks, public transport, and the array of shops which many of us take for granted, like video shops, take-away outlets, and service stations.

Be wary of developers and estate agents who say things like, "it's too good an opportunity to miss."

If it really is that good, they should have bought a property there. When I was an estate agent I was surprised by how many estate agents gave advice and made recommendations as though they were experts, yet did not purchase any real estate. To be a consultant, you should have first-hand experience in that field.

The qualities that I look for in a suburb in which to buy an investment property are:

- close to the city (but not in the city)
- close to beaches and bays, or rivers and lakes
- excellent public transport
- proximity to reputable schools and universities
- an abundance of cafés and restaurants
- fully developed, with no large parcels of land available for development

The city's neighbour

The reason I look for suburbs close to the city is simply proximity to most people's place of work. People do not want to commute for hours each day to get to work. This is why residential suburbs near the city have always been popular.

Residential suburbs are not the only ones close to cities. Typically, some inner suburbs also comprise large industrial areas. But as cities grow and more people work within them, demand for housing in nearby suburbs also grows. Because of this, large industrial suburbs near cities are cleaned up, factories are closed down and moved to outer areas where land prices are cheaper, and inner suburbs are re-zoned to permit more residential housing. This demand has also led to a boom in residential apartment accommodation within cities.

I prefer to look in suburbs near the city, because cities have no building height restrictions. This means there is no limit to the possible number of apartments for sale. If you own an inner city apartment and a glut of new apartments are built so that supply exceeds demand, the resale price of your property would be adversely affected.

No building height restrictions also mean that the excellent outdoor views that add value to many inner city apartments can rarely be guaranteed. The apartment you paid top dollar for because of its wonderful view may one day have a view of a neighbouring concrete wall. This rarely happens in blue-chip suburbs because they have much tighter planning restrictions, including control over building heights.

Esprit de corps increases capital growth

I have also found that in blue-chip suburbs, residents take a much keener interest in local affairs. Because residents want to preserve the value of their homes and maintain their lifestyle and community spirit, they are much more likely to object to new housing applications.

Residents of blue-chip suburbs are also much more likely to start up groups like Save our Suburb, which lobby local councils to prevent the demolition of historic homes, the removal of established flora and fauna, and the reduction of recreational open space like parks and reserves. These groups are better informed about council planning schemes, making new development more difficult.

I look for suburbs no more than fifteen kilometres from the city centre. I believe this distance is not excessive for people to commute to the city for work, and within this radius I have a huge number of suburbs to choose from.

Go near the water

The second feature I look for when investing in a suburb is proximity to water, like an ocean, river, or lake.

Historically, most major cities were established where there was good access to water to allow for trade. The better suburbs are established near the water and the more respectable businesses of that time.

Water has always drawn our interest. Children always want to play in water, and we usually spend our holidays near water. Water is increasingly becoming our most important and vital resource. People love living near it. Many blue-chip residential suburbs within fifteen kilometres of the city centre are well known for their proximity to the bay, rivers, or lakes.

Ideally, I would like to own residential investment properties in all of these suburbs.

Public transport and proximity to schools

Another important consideration is public transport. People renting tend to be young. In fact, a number of my tenants are students. They rely very much on public transport.

These tenants will only consider renting a property near their school. The blue-chip suburbs I look in are usually older areas, just like most renowned schools and universities are old ones. It is not a coincidence that these facilities tend to be located in or near blue-chip suburbs.

Restaurants and cafés

I also look in suburbs that have fine restaurants and fashionable cafés. Blue-chip suburbs tend to have these businesses because the residents that live there have a high disposable income. These restaurants and cafés attract a desirable clientele both to their business and to the area in general. Many young professionals want to live where they play.

A well-established suburb

The final point I look for in a suburb is that it should be fully developed and established, with no large areas left for further developments.

This is a very important point because it can affect the long-term capital growth in that area. In a particular year, blue-chip areas may not experience as much capital growth as a "hot spot", but they are always popular and there is always demand for housing.

If an area has high demand for housing and that demand cannot be met, it will create competition between buyers who are trying to buy the few properties that are available. This imbalance between supply and demand leads to capital growth.

In suburbs that still have large vacant areas available for development, developers will build new housing to satisfy demand, which does not assist capital growth in those areas.

Old port or industrial areas are a common example. These suburbs are also often within 15 km of the city centre and close to water, but still have room for development and are not considered blue-chip areas.

These areas are frequently redeveloped to allow residential housing to meet the demands of people who work in the city and want to live near work. The old factories and warehouses are demolished and new housing is built.

Such areas may be advertised as the new "hot spot", and they attract a lot of interest from prospective buyers. But because more and more properties are built to meet demand, the resale prices for already established homes in these areas can be adversely affected. Buyers do not need to compete with one another, because plenty of new homes are being built. When demand begins to wane, builders cut their prices to secure more sales.

This is why I look in fully developed areas, where competition between buyers will force home prices to rise.

Stamp duty

Deciding what type of property to buy was my next decision. Although I want a cross-section of properties, including new homes, established homes, period homes, townhouses, and apartments, I began by looking for properties for sale off the plan. In my state, I would save a substantial amount of money on stamp duty by buying off the plan.

Some states calculate the stamp duty payable on the contract of sale price, whether the property has been built or not. The stamp duty where my properties are located is calculated on the value of the property at the time of the sale. Therefore, if I buy a property off the plan before any construction work starts, stamp duty is payable only on the value of the land.

For instance, if I buy a property for $350,000, but the value of the land at the time I sign the contract of sale is only $80,000, the stamp duty payable is approximately $1700. If the same $350,000 property were already built, the stamp duty would be approximately $16,700.

Stamp duty differs from state to state. Check with an estate agent or solicitor in your area to determine how stamp duty will be calculated on your purchases.

Buying off the plan

I started by buying investment properties off the plan because I saved on stamp duty. Buying off the plan does involve some risks, though.

One of the risks is that the property may never be built if there are not enough pre-sales to make the project viable.

Another risk is that the builder may change the floor plan after you sign the contract if the local council makes planning alterations. Sometimes finishes like tiles, carpets, and tap fittings change too if discontinued by the manufacturer.

These potential risks may seem unlikely. In fact, they are very common. Many residential projects have been delayed or terminated due to insufficient pre-sales, or because the cost of construction has increased to the point where the project is no longer profitable.

Generally, the success of large-scale residential developments is based on the number of sales made before construction commences. When developers borrow money to start a new project, finance companies require that a certain percentage of the development is pre-sold, thereby ensuring that there is a demand for the product.

Developers need to pre-sell up to 60 percent of the project to secure funds to start construction.

This percentage will vary depending on the size of the development, the amount borrowed, and the projected completion date for the project.

The real estate market can change quickly, and so can the cost of building materials. Many projects are shelved because of this. If this happens, the purchaser should not incur any financial loss and payments should be refunded in full. But even if you haven't lost financially, you have lost an opportunity to start or expand your property portfolio.

It may be a long time between when you sign the contract and when the development is terminated and your money is refunded. That time cannot be refunded, and time is what is needed to allow an investment to grow. Therefore if you have purchased a property in a development that does not proceed, you have definitely suffered a loss.

It may also seem unlikely that the floor plan or finishes of a property purchased off the plan can change after you have signed a contract. From my experience, though, this is also quite common.

All the contracts I have seen relating to properties for sale off the plan include clauses that permit the developer to make alterations if the need arises. Usually these clauses allow the developer to make only minor alterations, either to the plan, or to the construction work. Under these clauses the developer may make alterations without reference to the purchaser, and without affecting the price paid for the property.

It is crucial to have a solicitor read your contract and point out pertinent clauses before you sign. Contracts for properties off the plan are usually enormous, and I certainly do not have the inclination or legal knowledge to read and fully understand these documents. A solicitor will inform you of your legal rights if any problems occur.

Buying established homes

A major benefit of buying an established home, rather than a property off the plan, is that you can see exactly what you are buying.

For those buying off the plan for the first time, I recommend that you carefully compare the measurements of the property you are interested in with the room sizes of an already established home.

It is easy to assume when reading dimensions off a plan that rooms will be accommodating and the floor plan functional. Many buyers make this mistake, because most floor plans available to prospective buyers include pictures of furniture comfortably positioned in each room.

For example, a floor plan may include a nine square metre bedroom. To help create the illusion that this room is large, the drawing may show a bed with two pillows to give the impression that it is a double bed, with bedside tables on either side. It may even include an armchair in the corner. In fact, a nine square metre bedroom (a common bedroom size, particularly in smaller apartments) will only fit one single bed and one bedside table only.

A double bedroom should be a minimum of 3.5 × 4 metres.

The mistake can be easily avoided by comparing room measurements on a plan with the rooms in the buyer's own home. Unfortunately, many buyers discover after their property is complete that the building is far smaller than they imagined. Remember, furniture shown on floor plans is not usually drawn to scale.

Ceiling heights are another common trap. Few floor plans show the proposed ceiling height, and very few buyers ask. As a general rule higher ceilings are better. But the higher the ceiling is, the higher the overall construction costs will be.

Opting to go off the plan

I minimised these risks by looking for a project where construction had already begun.

With such a property I could reasonably assume that the developer had the financial means to complete the job, and I could inspect the partially completed property to get a better idea of how spacious it would be.

I would still save a lot on stamp duty. I would also receive the normal building guarantee for new homes (which in this case is seven years), and with a new home I would receive the maximum depreciation benefits at tax time. Most importantly, the pre-sales would be excellent comparable sales evidence to help me obtain a satisfactory independent valuation of the property.

I wanted a partially completed property because I knew that the completion date and settlement would be imminent. Often when buying properties off a plan, the expected completion and settlement date can be up to three years away. I had two reasons for wanting an imminent settlement date.

Firstly, I was anxious to start my property portfolio straight away. I did not want to wait for years before owning another property. Secondly, I did not want to risk the real estate market changing drastically between the time of purchasing and settling the property.

Many people, myself included, have purchased a property to be completed years after the purchase date, in the belief that the real estate market would improve between purchase and settlement. Of course the risk is that in that time the real estate market may actually decline, so that the purchase price is more than the property is worth at the time of settlement. This could leave you with a serious financial dilemma if you are borrowing money to buy the property.

A unique choice

Another feature I look for in an investment property is that it must be unique and in a boutique development. These are important characteristics if you decide to sell in the future. If you have a truly unique property it ensures that when you decide to sell you will not face stiff competition from other sellers.

A prospective buyer who likes your property will be compelled to negotiate with you. You are far more likely to secure a sale price that you are happy with. A boutique development—a small, exclusive development—will complement your unique property.

The problem with large developments is repetition. A residential apartment building comprising 20 levels can have up to 300 apartments. The architects will naturally design different apartment styles and sizes, but generally the same, or very similar, apartments are repeated over many levels. Often entire floors are repeated numerous times.

If the apartment you are selling is similar to many others in the same building, it is very likely that an apartment identical to yours will be for sale at the same time. This competition can have serious consequences on the price you receive.

Large-scale apartment buildings are bad for capital growth

Naturally any prospective buyer will want to buy the cheaper property, and they can offer each owner a low figure until one accepts. Even if one property is better furnished and presented, the buyer will usually purchase the cheaper property and then try and emulate the better finish and presentation. I do not believe large-scale residential apartment buildings are best suited to provide long-term capital growth.

... but good for renting

While I would not buy a property in one of these buildings, I would consider renting one. Many of these large developments offer residents facilities such as gymnasiums, pools and tennis courts. Living in one of these buildings can be a lot of fun. Generally residents have unlimited use of these facilities. The cost of maintaining pools, tennis courts, and the like, is paid for by the apartment owners through their body corporate contributions. A large percentage of these developments are sold to investors.

The competitive sale prices within these developments also make it difficult to secure high rental returns. At any given time there are usually a number of apartments available for rent, so prospective tenants can apply to rent several apartments at a low price.

For these reasons I do not look for investment properties in large-scale developments. Instead, I look for boutique developments with up to 20 truly unique, individually designed properties.

Bigger is often better

I look for an investment property at least fifty square metres in size and with a minimum of two bedrooms. The reason is that very few finance companies will lend money for properties that are less than fifty square metres. Likewise, it is very difficult to obtain finance to purchase a bed-sitter. The reason for this is simple.

Small properties attract very little capital growth. Of course, over time these properties will grow in value, but not usually at the same rate as the real estate market as a whole.

I look for properties with at least two bedrooms because I want to appeal to the largest pool of tenants possible. Very few people want to rent one-bedroom properties. Even single people living alone like to have a spare bedroom for storage or guests.

Naturally, if I sell a property, I also want to appeal to as many prospective buyers as possible, and buyers prefer at least two bedrooms for the same reasons as tenants do.

Covered off-street parking

Finally, I only choose properties that include covered off-street car parking. The areas in which I look have good public transport, but I believe a two-bedroom property should have at least one parking space. A property with three or more bedrooms should include at least two parking spaces. This means the property will appeal to as many prospective tenants as possible.

More and more new developments, particularly in or near the city, do not include car parking spaces. Demand for housing is great and consequently the pressure is high to squeeze as many properties as possible onto the available space. Often this means car parking spaces are sacrificed.

It is reasonable to assume that the majority of two- and three- bedroom rental properties will be rented by two tenants with one car. If I do not provide for these tenants, I limit my potential rental market.

I started by buying properties off the plan to save on stamp duty. If this saving had not been available in my state, I would have begun by looking for recently built properties with the above features. The main reasons for this are:

- you can see exactly what you are buying,
- new properties are always popular with tenants and easy to rent
- you receive maximum depreciation benefits.

My list of requirements, at a glance

My total list of requirements looks like this:

- a blue-chip area
- within 15 km of the city, but not in the CBD
- close to water
- good public transport
- close to reputable schools and universities
- near popular restaurants and cafes
- in a fully developed area
- new property, save on stamp duty and depreciation
- a boutique development, with 20 or fewer individually designed properties
- minimum two bedrooms
- car parking
- at least fifty square metres in size

It is very difficult to find a property that fits all these criteria, and I use it as a guide only. In the past I have made exceptions. However, I will only purchase an investment property if it has most of the characteristics I have listed.

As time passes and the real estate market and government legislation changes, I may add to or subtract from this list.

Why I sometimes depart from my criteria

As an example, the apartment I was living in at the start of this story is located in the city, where I do not usually look for properties. I will keep this apartment as a long-term investment, though, because it fits all my other requirements.

The apartment is in a boutique four-storey apartment building. The building itself has some historical characteristics. Each apartment includes sought-after features like high ceilings (over twelve feet), exposed beams and bulkheads. Some apartments are split-level and some have polished floors. All have been individually designed, ensuring that no two apartments are alike.

The property is close to parks, sporting venues, restaurants, universities, trams, and trains.

Likewise, many of my other properties do not fulfil all of my criteria I have set. Some properties

I have purchased are further away from the city than fifteen kilometres. One is a 3 bedroom plus study townhouse with only one car parking space. One apartment is in a building with more than twenty apartments.

I still chose to buy these properties because, like my inner city apartment, each property is unique. They are situated in boutique developments in desirable blue-chip suburbs.

Most importantly, as a result of these characteristics I believe that any of my properties would attract considerable interest from prospective purchasers.

Summary

- Look in established suburbs near the CBD and/or water. Avoid 'the next big thing'
- Buying off the plan saves on stamp duty, but check dimensions against your own home
- Construction that has already begun is a good guarantee
- Consider tenants' preferences
- A unique property is good for capital growth

11. The Syndicate

From knowing what you want to buy to actually going out and buying it can seem like a gigantic and often daunting leap of faith.

I had a plan that I thought was simple. I wanted to buy a good, desirable property in a blue-chip suburb at a genuine discount price. My plan was to buy in bulk and receive a discount, just as many people do with almost anything from cars to movie tickets.

Consumers take advantage of these discounts every day, perhaps without even realising it. Supermarkets commonly offer a third item for free when you buy two items, or you might go to the theatre with friends and receive a discount for a group booking. Whatever the value of the product, most retailers are happy to sell something for less per item if they can thereby sell greater quantities.

Discounts do not just apply to products. They can also apply to services like dry cleaners, hairdressers, or car washes. The more you use these services, the less you pay per visit.

This is a simple concept that I was comfortable with. I can receive a discount when buying Coca-Cola in bulk, so why not get a discount for buying houses in bulk?

Some readers will not be comfortable with the idea of buying numerous properties at one time, particularly when just starting their property portfolio. This chapter is about how I bought properties in bulk because chronologically this is how my investment portfolio began. Later, I give examples of how I bought homes individually.

Some readers' journeys begin at this chapter. Others will begin at page one. Some readers will want to begin by finding out how to buy individual properties. Where readers begin their journey is not important. I want to give information and ideas that all readers can relate to, and which will help them reach their goals.

I am rather conservative. I did not want to buy multiple properties at once and risk over-committing myself and being unable to settle the properties. I therefore invited some close friends and my younger brother to join me and form a syndicate.

An eclectic group

It was an eclectic group, with vastly different backgrounds and ideas. One friend is ultra-conservative, one is exceedingly optimistic, one prays a lot, and one is always late. Two of my friends bought the home that they live in, while the other two had never purchased any real estate.

None of them had any current practical real estate knowledge, but they were all keen to find out how they could buy investment properties. We started off meeting once a week at a pub to discuss strategies.

Initially we achieved very little, but we had a lot of fun. My ultra-conservative friend acted as secretary, bringing paper, folders, hole punch and pens to each meeting. He was so enthusiastic about 'spreadsheeting' everything that it became our ongoing joke, but we were all grateful that he was so methodical.

My optimistic friend was always ready for action, he just wasn't sure what to do. And despite the fact that every week we met at the same pub at the same time, my brother was always late—even though he managed the pub.

How we started

We each came up with a list of five blue-chip sub-urbs where they would like to buy an investment property. Each person would look for suitable properties under construction in the suburbs they chose and report back to the group.

Unfortunately this led to pandemonium. Potentially suitable developments were everywhere and we were travelling large distances to check each site. Some friends knew an area well while others did not, and reaching any agreement was becoming increasingly difficult. The situation was becoming unmanageable.

We decided to concentrate all our efforts into one suburb. We met there each weekend over the next couple of months. We divided the suburb up into smaller areas. Each person was responsible for driving along every street in their area. We would record any properties we might want to buy, as well as any that looked recently built, which we could use as a price comparison.

We were looking for a medium size unit or townhouse development still under construc-tion. We found a number of projects, but dis-missed most of them for a variety of reasons. They backed onto railway tracks, or the road was too busy and so on.

We did find one suitable development and ascertained the price, size, builder, anticipated completion date, and all the other relevant information.

Comparing prices

We then compared recent sale prices for properties of comparable size in the area, checking sales results published in newspapers and online, and asking local estate agents. These sources gave us the sales results of most of the recently built comparable properties we had noticed driving around the suburb.

Most properties comparable to the ones we were interested in sold for around $330,000 or slightly above. After driving along every street in the suburb and obtaining dozens of comparable sales, we were confident that we could obtain an independent valuation for them of $330,000 each.

Our goal was to buy the properties with a minimum 5 percent discount. Based on our expectation that we could achieve a valuation of $330,000 each, we agreed that we could offer as high as $313,500 for each property.

We wanted at least a 5 percent discount because most banks, including the major banks, will lend up to 95 percent of the sale price or the independent valuation figure. If we could obtain a loan of 95 percent against the independent valuation figure—assuming that the townhouses would be valued at $330,000—we would then only have to pay stamp duty, legal costs and bank fees. We estimated these costs would total only a few thousand dollars.

Our first attempt

The development we were interested in comprised four two-storey three-bedroom two-bathroom townhouses with double garages, approximately five hundred metres from the beach and less than fifteen kilometres from the city. The asking price was $340,000 each.

I met the estate agent who was handling the sale. I knew I could offer up to $313,500 for each townhouse, but I started off by offering $1.2 million for all four townhouses, the equivalent of $300,000 per townhouse. I did this to show the agent I was a bona fide buyer and also to try to get him to work for us.

Commission

Estate agencies usually receive a commission of 2–3 percent of the value of the property. Of this amount, the individual agent who handled the listing and sale of the property receives 40–45 percent of the gross commission.

Therefore, if the commission payable on the townhouses we were interested in was 2.5 percent of the property's value, the estate agency would make $30,000 (for selling all four townhouses) and of this amount the agent whom I was speaking with would receive about $13,000.

It was unlikely that the estate agent I was meeting with would be able to mentally calculate this within the few seconds he had before the negotiations continued, but he would have realised his earnings for that month would be considerably better if we purchased the townhouses.

An estate agency may not have exclusive authority to market and sell properties. If this is the case, and it usually is with developments like the one we were considering, the estate agency would receive commission only for buyers they introduced to the property.

Most estate agents are entirely commission-based salespeople, who receive a nominal weekly allowance to help pay for some of their costs associated with running a car. If an estate agent does not sell anything they will very quickly go broke. Because of this, agents work just as hard to convince vendors to accept lower prices as they do persuading purchasers to pay higher prices, although agents are employed and paid by vendors.

A potential ally

Construction had only recently begun on the townhouses we were interested in, so it was unlikely that the development had been marketed very much. The estate agent certainly had not opened the houses for inspection. Like any commission-based sales person, he would have realised that our deal could make him a handsome sum of money for very little effort.

For these reasons, an estate agent can be a great ally in your endeavours to buy investment properties.

We haggled. I told the agent I represented a group of professional investors and could not offer a higher price without their authorization. The estate agent said he believed the properties would sell for more. I didn't argue. Instead, I pointed out that to do so, they would need to be marketed, which would incur costs for the vendor and require time and effort from the agent, with no guarantee of success.

I then produced sales evidence of similar townhouses that had sold in the area for around $300,000.

Earlier in this book, I mentioned that there will always be properties that have sold both above and below your desired price. How you choose to use this information is crucial.

I showed this information to the estate agent, not to try and persuade him that our offer was fair, but to demonstrate that we were discerning buyers making a reasonable offer based on factual sales evidence. The vendor would be taking a risk by declining our offer.

Everybody benefits from a reasonable offer

By accepting our offer, the vendor would have secured sales. Once the townhouses were complete, settlement could take place without delay. The developers would have minimised interest charges on any money they have borrowed. They could confidently plan their next project, which after all is how developers make money.

If completed properties remain for sale for an

extended period of time, the cost to the vendor can be significant. The saving in marketing costs alone usually amounts to about 1 percent of the value of the property.

Negotiating

When negotiating it is very important not to get emotional. The decision to make an offer on a particular property, and the level of the offer, is a business decision. If you cannot buy the property for the right price you will find other suitable properties.

Although the estate agent will most likely be familiar with your comparable sales evidence, it is still in your best interests to show him. By doing this, you demonstrate your thoroughness, you remind the agent of sales he may have forgotten, you imply that your first offer is your final offer, and you give the agent information which will encourage the vendor/s to accept your offer.

Estate agents work just as hard getting vendors to accept less for their home as they do trying to get purchasers to pay more. Even if the estate agent says things like "I needn't present your offer because the owner would be insulted", do not apologise, and do not take the bait and increase your offer on the spot. Whatever your offer, and whatever the estate agent might say, your offer will be submitted to the vendors.

Agents and vendors

Estate agents pass on all offers to the vendors for three reasons:

- They are compelled by law to submit all offers to their vendors.
- They need to show the vendor that they are working the property and submitting buyers.
- Most importantly, they are conditioning the vendor. Submitting low offers makes the vendor far more likely to accept a reasonable offer, even if it is a bit lower than their initial expectations.

Estate agents will also pass on comparable sales evidence to vendors, to try and persuade the owner that their home may be worth less then they might have been hoping for, without being responsible for the information.

Why listed prices are so high,
and how that helps you

In Australia, commission is entirely paid by the seller. The buyer pays nothing. Because of this system, estate agents have their own rule: *if you control the listings, you control the money.* This fundamental necessity to list every home possible to ensure you can earn a living creates fierce competition between estate agents.

To secure these listings, some agents will give vendors an inflated assessment of what their property is worth in the current market. Naturally, most vendors use the agent who gives them the highest valuation. As a result, many homes are initially listed at far too high a price and agents often need to condition vendors to accept less. This means that agents are usually grateful for any offer.

Estate agents are people too

Of course, estate agents are just people and if the estate agent likes you, your offer will be presented more favourably. It is therefore in your best interests to put up as few barriers as possible when making an offer. Be punctual when meeting the agent. Don't argue with them. Listen to them, and then give your response calmly.

Your meeting with the estate agent is a business meeting, so act and dress accordingly. Try to appear confident but friendly. Don't be aggressive or arrogant.

Remember that you want the agent to work for you.

Terms and conditions

Terms can play just as important a role as price. For instance, one vendor may be able to vacate and settle a property when you want, while others may want a quicker settlement. If the terms and conditions attached to an offer are unacceptable it may prevent a sale, even if the price is right.

I wanted our offer to have the greatest chance of success.

I submitted an unconditional offer, with a flexible settlement to suit the vendor. This may not always be possible, as you must be absolutely sure you can settle the property. If, for example, you are not completely sure that you can get finance, you should always make your offer subject to finance.

Some common conditions that appear on sale contracts are:

- Subject to a satisfactory
  building inspection
- Subject to a pest inspection
- Subject to the buyer's home selling

'Subject to the buyer's home selling' is very rarely accepted by vendors. Usually the period of time involved is too long, and there is a good chance that the sale will not proceed.

If possible, I recommend making an unconditional offer on a flexible settlement. The terms will definitely be acceptable to the vendor.

Another buyer may be offering for the same property at the same time. In these cases, vendors may prefer a lower but unconditional offer to a higher offer that is subject to conditions.

If you don't get your desired outcome

I didn't need to meet with the estate agent for very long because I made it clear I could not negotiate, as I was making an offer on behalf of a group of investors. The next day the agent told me the vendor had declined our offer.

Unfortunately I did not receive a counter-offer from the vendor. A counter-offer is a figure that the vendor would accept. I had hoped for a counter-offer below $340,000. Because I did not receive a counter-offer at all, I could only assume that our offer was a long way from acceptable.

I phoned the estate agent the following day to make another appointment. I increased our offer to $1,254,000, which was the equivalent of $313,500 per unit. This was our upper limit. The initial offer of $1.2 million was $160,000 below the asking price, so there would be no benefit in increasing our offer by only $5,000 or $10,000. I emphasised that $1.254 million was our final offer. I also re-iterated that if we were unsuccessful we would look elsewhere.

The next day our increased offer was also declined. This time the vendor did make a counter-offer of $330,000 per unit, just the amount at which we had valued these properties. This may have been a fair market price, but it did not give us the discount we set out to achieve. I started to doubt my initial idea to buy in bulk.

... try again

Shortly after our first failure, perhaps in answer to his prayers, my friend saw a new townhouse development. This development also comprised two-storey townhouses near the beach and city, but there were fourteen townhouses in this development. We acquired all the relevant information and discovered that eight of the townhouses had already sold.

The townhouses had quite similar designs. The two options were a three-bedroom, two-bathroom, double garage, fifteen square townhouse, or a slightly larger version with a study. Only the facades, colour schemes and landscaping differed. The development was situated in a highly sought-after area, and we decided that with its high, decorative powered security gates, it was exclusive and boutique enough for us.

I asked the estate agent who was selling the townhouses what the other eight had sold for. I did not mention our syndicate, because I wanted to give the appearance that any negotiations would be straightforward.

I needed to be sure that the prices had not increased as the project neared completion. This is common with these types of developments, because usually at this stage developers have covered most of their costs and the last remaining townhouses represent profit. Properties in the first stages of a project are often sold for less to encourage sales. As demand for the remaining properties increases, so do their prices.

I reminded the agent that settling six properties is far more difficult than settling one. To get a loan, I would need to satisfy the bank that I had not paid too much for the houses. Eventually the bank would find out what the first eight townhouses had sold for through their valuer. If they had sold for less than I was prepared to pay, the bank might not finance my offer.

In about six months, information including the sale price would be available from the PRISM system, which is maintained by the Valuer General's office. Licensed users, such as valuers and estate agents, have access to this information.

I told the estate agent that I could eventually find out the sales prices by checking the PRISM system, but I was prepared to buy the townhouses now. The agent told me the first eight townhouses all sold within the first month of being listed for sale, to owner-occupiers. The sale prices looked like this:

No. 1 Three bedroom plus study townhouse. Sold for $490,191.

No. 2 Three bedroom townhouse. Sold for $420,726.

No. 3 Three bedroom townhouse. Sold for $430,000.

No. 7 Three bedroom townhouse. Sold for $415,000.

No. 8 Three bedroom townhouse. Sold for $420,000.

No. 12 Three bedroom plus study townhouse. Sold for $440,000.

No. 13 Three bedroom townhouse. Sold for $430,000.

No. 14 Three bedroom plus study townhouse. Sold directly by the developer to a relative for an undisclosed price.

No. 3 Three bedroom townhouse. Re-sold two months later for $446,000.

After receiving this information, we still re-searched comparable sales in the surrounding area. The remaining six townhouses would prob-ably sell relatively quickly, for close to the asking prices. We believed we could reasonably obtain independent valuations of $430,000 for the 3 bed-room townhouses and $440,000 for the three-bed-room plus study townhouses.

We believed that these prices were fair and rea-sonable, but we still wanted at least a 5 percent discount.

Accordingly we were prepared to make an offer for all six properties, but we would only offer as high as $408,500 for the three-bedroom townhous-es and $418,000 for the slightly larger townhouses. Six properties remained: three with a study and three without. We would offer up to $2,479,665 for all six.

I adopted the same approach as for the first development we were interested in. I offered the agent $2.4 million, based on a purchase price of $395,000 for the smaller townhouses and $405,000 for the larger townhouses. Just like in our first at-tempt, the agent told me that the offer was too low, and he had the comparable sales evidence within the development to prove it.

At this point I informed him of our syndicate. I told him I could not act without the authorisation of the syndicate, who, as discerning buyers, were only interested if they could receive a discount for buying in bulk. I did not refer to any sales results, because the developer clearly knew what the townhouses were worth. After all, eight had already sold.

I did not try to persuade the agent that the townhouses were only worth what we were prepared to offer. Instead, I pointed out the ongoing costs that would be incurred, the additional time and effort for the agent and developer, and the possibility that the six townhouses would not sell for more than our offer.

Our success or failure depended only on whether the developer would be satisfied with selling the remaining six properties for $2.4 million and moving on to the next project.

Results!

Our offer was declined, but this time the vendor made a counter-offer. If our syndicate bought all six townhouses, the vendor would accept $2.55 million. I increased our offer to $2.45 million. We finally settled on a figure of $2.48 million, or $408,500 for the smaller townhouses and $420,000 for the larger townhouses.

We were delighted with this result. For each of us, this was the beginning of our investment property portfolio.

When we formed the syndicate, we all agreed that we would individually sign sale contracts and purchase properties in our own names. This meant each of us could buy one townhouse, with one left over. We sold the sixth property for $427,500.

Buying in bulk is a technique I have used on many occasions, and results like this can be easily achieved. The methodology and negotiating techniques are exactly the same regardless of property value.

The discount you want to receive for buying properties, in bulk or individually, depends on the strength of the real estate market at the time. The weaker the market, the larger the discount you want. In strong markets it is difficult to negotiate large discounts, because competition between buyers forces prices to rise. When we bought these townhouses, the real estate market was extremely strong. For example, Townhouse No. 3 initially sold for $430,000 and two months later sold again for $446,000.

Before any negotiations commence you must have a clear picture of exactly what you want to achieve, and you must have carried out extensive research to find out what properties have sold for in the area you are looking in. Remember if you are unsuccessful, another property is just around the corner.

Summary

- You can get a discount for buying properties in bulk, too
- Compare prices
- Agents work just as hard to get vendors to accept lower prices
- Negotiate confidently and courteously
- Acceptable terms can influence a vendor to accept a lower price
- Know what you can offer and what you want to achieve

12. Deposit Bonds

After we signed the sale contracts we needed to pay deposits. A deposit is usually 10 percent of the purchase price. The primary purpose of a deposit is to provide a consideration to make the sale contract binding. The deposit also shows you are a genuine buyer. Most importantly, if you are in breach of the sale contract, your deposit will be paid to the vendor.

In my experience, very few purchasers question the amount of the deposit, or request a smaller deposit than the usual ten percent. When a purchaser has requested a smaller deposit, though, I have rarely known a vendor to refuse.

You don't have to pay a 10 percent deposit

The deposit the purchaser pays is held in a trust account, either by the vendor's estate agent or solicitor. In most cases the vendor will not receive this money until the property has settled, at which time they will receive the full proceeds from the sale. So, it does not usually matter whether the purchaser pays a smaller deposit, as long as it is enough to compensate the vendor if the contract is breached.

With the six townhouses, and all of my purchases since then, I requested a smaller deposit. I waited until the price had been agreed upon, because requesting a smaller deposit at the beginning may have looked like we could not afford to buy the properties.

When an estate agent asks me why I will not pay a 10 percent deposit, I tell them the deposit I am proposing is sufficient to demonstrate that I am a genuine buyer and to be adequate security for the vendor. I also tell them I cannot pay the deposit in cash. Instead, I provide a bank guarantee or deposit bond.

How guarantees and bonds work

I used guarantees and bonds when I bought my first investment properties. At the time I really could not afford a 5 percent deposit, let alone a 10 percent deposit, and I could not afford to lose a deposit of any size.

A bank guarantee or deposit bond can be used to buy a home instead of cash. A guarantee and a bond are essentially the same in what they provide. Both guarantee that if a purchaser is in breach of the sale contract, the company who issued the guarantee or bond will pay the agreed deposit to the vendor in full.

Of course, if this happens the company providing the guarantee will then seek reimbursement from the purchaser.

While the function of these instruments is essentially the same, the way in which they are issued is very different. To get a bank guarantee you must prove that you are able to settle the property, and only banks issue them. Deposit bonds are not issued by banks and you do not have to prove that you can settle the property. Instead, you must show that you have assets worth five times the value of the bond.

Guarantees and bonds are wonderful tools, designed specifically for people who are asset rich but cash poor. They are ideal for people who have money in their own home, the share market, term deposits and the like.

The costs

Guarantees and bonds are not free and the cost, like the application criteria, varies greatly between companies. Numerous companies now provide these types of deposits. The cost depends on the size of the deposit and the length of time before the property is settled and the guarantee or bond can be terminated.

Generally, I have found bank guarantees cheaper than deposit bonds, but harder to obtain. Although the cost for this type of deposit can seem expensive, it is usually not much more than you would pay if you borrowed the deposit money (taking into account the interest that would be charged and the establishment costs for a loan).

A deposit paid in cash earns no interest, sitting in a solicitor's or estate agent's trust account waiting for settlement.

Getting our guarantors

Because we could not prove to the bank that we could settle the townhouses, we had to use deposit bonds. Each of us needed assets worth five times the value of the bond, which we did not have.

The answer was to find people with assets who would be prepared to be our guarantors. This means if the deposit bond was paid to the vendor because we were in breach of the sale contract, the company who issued the bond could secure the assets of the guarantor to ensure that they could retrieve their money.

We approached family and friends. Not surprisingly, we met a lot of trepidation, but in the end our parents agreed to guarantee us. To prove that their homes (which were used to secure our bonds) were safe, we provided personal agreements. These allowed our parents to secure any of our assets to meet any financial obligations relating to the bonds.

This personal agreement may seem like little comfort, because we did not have the assets to secure the deposit bonds by ourselves. But it gave our parents enough confidence to be our guarantors.

The vendor is only entitled to the deposit

If a purchaser is in breach of a sale contract, the vendor is only entitled to receive the agreed deposit stated in the contract. So for a $400,000 property with a 5 percent deposit ($20,000), you will need assets worth $100,000 to get a deposit bond. However, if the purchaser breaches the sale contract the vendor will still only receive $20,000. The company that issued the bond will seize assets worth $20,000 belonging to the purchaser (or guarantor).

Purchasers must show assets worth five times the amount of the bond because:

- some assets are easier to liquidate than others (for instance term deposits are easier to liquidate than shares, and shares are easier than real estate),
- the value of the assets may decrease after the bond is issued
- some assets may be disposed of after the bond is issued.

Even though our assets were not enough to fully reimburse our parents if the deposit was paid to the vendor, we did have some of the deposit and we would repay any shortfall until the debt was repaid in full.

Gratitude is good business practice

We also paid our parents a small fee for agreeing to let us use their homes (their only major asset) as security for our bonds. Although this money was unsought, we wanted to further demonstrate our belief that their homes would be safe, and we wanted to show our own commitment and professionalism.

As children, we constantly take from our parents without much thought to the sacrifices they make. We have often received unconditional gifts and blessings from our parents with little thought or recognition.

We did not want our parents to think of us as ungrateful children they were propping up. Instead, we wanted to be viewed as professional investors who genuinely believed in what we were doing. Although the amount we paid was not large, it was enough to show that we appreciated that they were showing faith in us by letting us use the home they worked hard to pay off over the last 20–25 years.

The money we paid to our parents, together with the solicitor-approved personal agreement, didn't just reassure our parents about their homes. It also showed that we were taking a professional approach to our investment portfolio.

To demonstrate our thoroughness, I showed our parents the comparable sales and other research we had collected relating to the townhouses. I then went through the negotiation process with them. Finally, I showed them my financial report for my inner city apartment, to give them an idea of the work we were still going to do to ensure that we could settle the properties. I explained the entire process so that they would feel comfortable.

Ex gratia payments to family or friends may seem like a lot of money when added to the cost of deposit bonds or insurance, but the amount you pay family or friends is up to you. It is most important not to lose sight of your ultimate goal.

In this instance, we were each buying a townhouse for over $400,000. Without our parents' help, we would still be dreaming about our first investment property. The amount we paid for a bond plus the payment to our parents was insignificant compared to what we could make in the long term.

Our syndicate agreed it would be better to pay a nominal amount for a deposit bond and a nominal amount to our parents than to save that money and go without an investment property.

This proved to be one of the best decisions we made.

Since bank guarantees and deposit bonds have become widely available, it has become much easier for people to use the equity in one property to buy another property. Once you have a property it is relatively easy to get a bond or guarantee for another property. With every new property you buy the next property becomes easier to secure.

How to build a portfolio without spending your own money

If you are able to buy a property for the right price, you use a guarantee or bond for the deposit, and you borrow the remaining funds, it is possible to buy a property using very little of your own money. This is how many astute investors buy more and more investment properties without touching money in their private savings accounts.

Although I needed my parents' assistance for my first two investment properties, the equity in those two properties was enough to get my next bond, which secured the next investment property. Now the equity from every new property I buy helps me get the bond and bank finance for my next investment property.

Summary

- A deposit smaller than 10 percent is fine, as long as it is big enough for the vendor's security
- Bank guarantees require proof you can settle. Deposit bonds require assets five times the bond's value
- Treat your guarantors with professional courtesy and plan for disaster
- Once you own a property, you can use the equity to buy your next

13. Finance

Before approaching any banks to arrange finance for the townhouses we had purchased, we needed to prepare our financial reports.

The information included in the financial report was detailed in chapter 7, "The financial report". The financial reports for our new townhouses were similar in format, but the order in which we gathered the information had changed.

Get an independent valuation last

This time, we left the independent valuation for last. We wanted to show the valuer the information we had collected, to demonstrate our thoroughness and help persuade him that the townhouses were worth more than we had paid. We also wanted to show him that we required a higher valuation for bank finance, not in order to sell the properties.

Our other reason was to allow the real estate market time to grow as much as possible between when we signed the sale contracts and when the townhouses were re-valued. The more time that passes between these two events, the easier it is to argue that the real estate property market has shifted.

One important item of evidence that the market has shifted are newspaper articles. Even in a depressed market, there are usually good news stories talking the market up. Collect as many of these articles as possible, to show that there are positive indicators in the real estate market since you purchased your property and into the future.

Include existing investment properties

The only new section in my financial report is a section for my existing investment properties. I include colour brochures with internal and external photographs of each property, together with a description of the property and a copy of the floor-plan on the back. These brochures are very similar to those estate agents hand out to prospective purchasers at open for inspections.

I include these brochures to add colour to the report, and to show the bank managers what my investment properties look like. Information concerning the value of these properties is contained in my personal balance sheet (section 1 of the financial report).

The power of pictures

Although the financial information regarding my latest acquisition is far more important than colour brochures, I have found that bank managers invariably return to the colour brochures. Beyond being pleasing to the eye, colour brochures effectively show the result of all the words and numbers in my report.

A picture can often say more than words and attractive colour brochures usually elicit more conversation from an otherwise bored bank manager than all the financial information I have compiled.

However, the financial analysis is the heart of the financial report and will largely determine whether you can or cannot get bank finance. Therefore, while I include them for their eye-catching quality, I spend very little time on the colour brochures when I go through the financial report with a bank manager.

The valuer

Based on the information we had collected, we reassessed what we hoped to achieve from the independent valuation. We now thought a figure closer to mid $400,000 might be possible.

I went through all the information we had collected with the valuer, including comparable sales, depreciation schedules, rental appraisals, and a draft financial analysis. I completed the draft analysis with a valuation figure of $450,000.

I wanted to show the valuer what we believed the properties were worth and how this outcome would affect how the properties were geared.

If we were able to obtain a valuation at this level, and secured 90 percent bank finance, the properties would be neutrally geared before tax and positively geared after tax (assuming that the properties were rented for approximately $10 a week less than the rental estimates.)

I included all this information to help build rapport and trust with the valuer. I wanted to show that we wanted a higher valuation to settle the properties, not to sell them. Shortly after our meeting, the value of the townhouses was assessed at $455,000.

The importance of equity

This result effectively increased the equity we had in the townhouses. We purchased the smaller townhouses for $408,500 and the larger townhouses for $420,000. The independent valuation showed that we had equity of $46,500 (10.2 percent) in the smaller townhouses and $35,000 (7.7 percent) in the larger townhouses, assuming that our borrowings matched our purchase price.

If renting a home and buying your first investment property, your financial report should include all the sections listed in chapter 7.

If you already own a home or are paying off a home, regardless of whether you live in that home or it is an investment property, your financial report should include the following:

- Personal balance sheet
- Detailed financial analysis
- Copy of independent bank valuation
- Copy of quantity surveyor's report
- Brochures of property portfolio
- Twelve-month rental estimates
- Salary confirmation
- Individual credit report
- Comprehensive insurance cover
- Evidence of comparable sales

Applying for our loan

After achieving the independent valuation figure we wanted and completing the financial report, I met with the bank manager. Because all our reports were very similar, initially only I met with the manager. All five of us at once might talk over one another and create a bad impression.

Before meeting the manager I called the bank and told them I wished to apply for a loan for $2.4 million. I did this to ensure that I would meet with the manager, not a clerk. As before, I went through each section of the financial report with the manager for the townhouse I was purchasing.

I did not bring the reports for the other five townhouses. Instead, I explained, each member of our syndicate would meet individually with the manager, but only if he believed our loan applications were likely to be successful. Of course, the manager would not make any guarantees about the success or failure of our loans until he could meet with each of us separately and consider our financial reports. However, based on my report and our initial meeting he acknowledged that he thought the deal looked promising and he could see no reason why our loans would not be approved.

Keep your options open

I also met with a second bank. During this meeting I made the second bank manager aware that I had also met with their competition, and our syndicate would only give our business to their bank if they approved all our loan applications, not just a few. Finally, we would not allow the banks to check our individual credit report until they had approved our loans in principle. The individual credit report was the last check required.

We applied to both banks for loans equivalent to 90 percent of the independent valuation figure. If successful, this would enable us to get a loan of $409,500, which would fully cover the purchase price of the smaller three-bedroom townhouses, and nearly account for the purchase price of the larger three-bedroom plus study townhouses.

The size of the loan you require for each property will depend upon the size of the discount you are able to negotiate, and on your individual financial position. Some readers will be able to borrow 95 percent of the independent valuation figure, while others will not. From our conversations with the banks, we decided that we would have a better chance of success if we applied for a 90 percent loan.

On some occasions I have applied for and received loans equivalent to 95 percent of the valuation figure. But I usually applied for a 95 percent loan with one bank and a 90 percent loan with a second bank. If both loans are approved, I use the bank that will give me the most money. If the 95 percent loan is refused, the second loan application for 90 percent is there as a back-up.

After my initial meeting with the bank managers and in their belief that our loan applications would probably be approved, each member of our syndicate individually made a time to meet with the managers. Once our applications were lodged, we could do nothing more than wait.

A few months before purchasing our townhouses, my brother spoke with his bank and enquired how much he could borrow to buy a home. He had not found a home at that stage, but as many first home buyers do, he made an appointment with the bank to see what price bracket he should begin looking in.

He was informed that he could borrow $100,000 based on his salary and the deposit he had saved. My brother believed that was insufficient to buy a home in the areas he was interested in. Immediately after he expressed his disappointment, the bank had a change of heart and advised him that he could borrow $150,000. He left the bank a little happier.

Now, a few short months later, each person in our syndicate, including my brother, was applying for a loan in excess of $400,000. It was not surprising that we were all a little anxious.

A few nervous days passed, and finally we received the news we had hoped for. Our loans for 90 percent of the independent valuation figure had been approved. If relief made an audible sound, we could have held a rock concert. After the good news we simply counted the days until settlement would occur and we would own our new investment property. Unfortunately though, all did not go well.

Mortgage insurance

Shortly before settlement was to take place, we were told that our loans would not be approved because of mortgage insurance.

Whenever you apply for a loan that exceeds 80 percent of the value of the security, you require mortgage insurance approval. If this is the case, the bank will apply for mortgage insurance on your behalf.

Based on our financial reports, the banks had assessed our applications and were happy to approve the loans. They then passed on our applications to the mortgage insurance company for assessment, incorrectly assuming that approval would be a formality.

The reason the bank was so confident was that the financial analysis showed the investment would be self-funding, meaning the rental income would pay the interest on the loan and all other costs associated with the property. The bank was satisfied the properties were worth more than we had paid, and they were happy with the amount of equity we had in the properties. Unfortunately, they incorrectly assumed the mortgage insurance company would come to the same conclusion.

Indeed, the bank was almost right. Based on our financial reports, the mortgage insurance company advised that normally they would approve the loans. However, their policy for properties which have not settled was that loan applications must be assessed on the purchase price or an independent valuation figure, whichever is the lower.

If we had applied for 90 percent of the purchase price, rather than 90 percent of the independent valuation figure, the mortgage insurance company would approve our loans. This would then enable us to borrow up to $367,650 for the smaller townhouses and $378,000 for the larger townhouses.

In an attempt to rectify the situation, the bank informed us that they would still be happy to lend us 80 percent of the independent valuation figure, but 80 percent of the valuation figure was less than what we could borrow with mortgage insurance approval.

Amounts borrowable with and without mortgage insurance

Property	Purchase price	Sworn valuation	Bank loan 90% w/ins.	Bank loan 80% no ins.
3 bedroom townhouse	$408,500	$455,000	$367,650	$364,000
3 bedroom plus study	$420,000	$455,000	$378,000	$364,000

Neither scenario was acceptable to us, because whichever loan we chose we did not have the extra $40,000–$50,000 required to settle the properties. Unfortunately, too much time had elapsed between receiving verbal confirmation that the loans were approved and being told we could not in fact borrow the money we needed. As a result it was too late to approach other banks and apply for loans, and if we delayed settlement we would incur stiff financial penalties.

Despondently, we had to accept one of the two loans being offered and then raise the extra money needed to settle.

We agreed that although the bank's 80 percent loan offered us less money than we could borrow with mortgage insurance approval, the bank's loans were preferable because we would save the cost of mortgage insurance, which was approximately $8,500.

Before accepting any loans, we met with the bank manager again to see if the bank had any other products that would allow us to borrow the extra funds. Unfortunately, there was nothing else they could do.

Be assertive

Our syndicate continued to mull over how we would raise the extra funds, and shortly after being assured that we could borrow no more money, we made another time to meet with the same bank manager. This time, rather than asking the bank what they could do, we told them what we needed.

We would accept the 80 percent bank loan, but the day after the townhouses settled, we would re-finance the properties with the same bank, and this time we would get a loan of 90 percent of the independent valuation figure. We were confident this would work because when we first applied for the 90 percent loans, the mortgage insurance company advised us that the loans would have been approved but for their policy of assessing our applications against the purchase price.

If we re-financed the properties the day after settlement, the mortgage insurance company would consider our loan of $364,000 versus an independent valuation of $455,000, and they would base their decision on the information contained in our financial reports.

The mortgage insurance company would not know that the properties settled the day before and our $364,000 loans were only one day old. The new loan applications would be assessed on their merits.

Don't delay!

The bank agreed, and to expedite matters they prepared the documents for re-financing the properties at the same time as preparing loan acceptance documents. On this basis we signed loan documents with the bank, but we still needed to raise the extra $40,000 to $50,000 for settlement to occur.

The settlement dates for the townhouses varied according to when the developer expected to complete them. Our syndicate pooled every bit of money we had—including getting cash advances on credit cards—to raise the funds needed to settle the first two townhouses. We then re-financed these two townhouses the day after settlement. Fortunately, we were correct. We received approval from the mortgage insurance provider for new 90 percent loans based on our independent valuation figures.

The new loans were approved and established just in time to enable us to use the money from the new, larger loans to settle the next two townhouses. Likewise, we immediately re-financed these two townhouses after settlement, but this time the new loans were not established in time to get the money required to settle the last two townhouses. We had to look for help outside our syndicate.

*Experience gives borrowers,
and lenders, confidence*

We borrowed money from family, friends, colleagues, bosses, and anyone else who would give us a short-term loan, however little. We had as many as nine loans from these sources, but we knew that once the properties settled, we could re-pay these people within a very short period. Our confidence and past results helped us raise the money required.

We settled the last two townhouses and then applied for re-financing. However, this time we only re-financed one townhouse because we sold the other while it was still under construction. As I explained in chapter 11, "The syndicate", we sold the sixth townhouse because it was surplus to our needs. As a result, we had a back-to-back settlement. We settled the townhouse and paid the developer $408,500 as agreed in our sale contract, and a few hours later we sold it, receiving $427,500.

We had achieved what we set out to do. We found boutique properties in a blue-chip area, purchased them at a genuine discount price, secured the townhouses using deposit bonds and then paid for them with the bank's money, and we used very little or none of our own money.

We had some scares along the way, and we created a mountain of paperwork for the bank by applying for a new loan just the day after receiving one loan, but the result justified the work involved.

Anything really is possible!

From my personal experiences, and after speaking with numerous people about this subject, I am now of the opinion that you can borrow an almost unlimited amount of money to buy investment properties.

Many readers would have seen or read stories in the media about battlers who have made good or housewives who in their spare time have bought investment properties worth millions. These property moguls may not be smarter than the average person, but they can form a persuasive argument and convince the banks that they have purchased a good investment.

Whatever the value of the property you are buying, if you can show that you have bought it at a genuine wholesale price—that is, below its true market value—and you can service the loan and all costs associated with the property, then you will be able to borrow money to purchase it. This applies even to million-dollar properties.

Non-residential investment properties

However, as I explained earlier, it is difficult to find tenants for a million-dollar home who can pay enough rent to fully cover a large loan. As a general rule, the more expensive a home, the smaller the rental return (when calculated as a percentage). This is not necessarily the case with other types of properties, such as warehouses, factories, and commercial properties.

I buy residential investment properties because I am passionate about this type of real estate. I can carry out extensive research on different suburbs, and I feel confident. I would not be comfortable or confident buying any other kind of real estate because I do not believe I know enough about this market.

However, I have met investors who have bought non-residential real estate worth millions of dollars with a single purchase. They bought these properties following a similar plan to the one I have described in this book. In principle, the purchase price is largely irrelevant provided that the investment makes good business sense.

If, for instance, you are able to find an investment property worth $1,000,000 for only $800,000, and the property has existing tenants with a long-term lease that will fully pay the bank loan and all other associated costs, very few banks would not lend you even this large amount. If the purchaser finds they cannot afford to keep the property, the bank can sell it.

Banks also have to consider their worst-case scenario, which is that the loan is not serviced. If this occurs, the bank needs to secure the property and sell it to retrieve their money. Therefore, in order to get a loan, you must show the bank that the investment property you are buying is worth considerably more than the bank's loan.

You can do this either by using your own money to help buy the property, or by using your negotiating skills to convince the bank.

Why some loans are declined

Because of this fundamental requirement that the property you are buying must be worth more than the bank loan, banks are becoming increasingly hesitant to tell people how much they can borrow before they buy a property.

I have already explained how you can buy a million-dollar property, but some readers may have previously applied for a much smaller loan and been declined.

There are two requirements for a loan, the loan versus asset value (which banks call L.V.R., loan-to-value ratio), and how the loan will be serviced.

Imagine someone wishing to buy a home to live in who is refused a loan for $200,000, but later successfully borrows $400,000 for an investment property.

One reason could be that the $200,000 loan was for a home that the bank valued at only $150,000. Or the bank may have refused the loan on the basis that the person's salary is too low to re-pay the loan.

Shortly afterwards that same person can borrow $400,000 for an investment property, if they have clearly shown that the asset they are buying is worth more than the loan, and the loan is being re-paid by the rental income their property is generating.

Every property you own is like a little business

As a rule, no bank will lend you money if they believe the asset is worth less than you have paid, unless you are using other assets as collateral to secure the loan.

An exception to this rule would be if you were borrowing the extra funds to improve the property, and thereby increase its value. If you have had a loan declined, it is important to forget any prejudices you might have.

Each investment property you buy is like a little business, with income and expenses. Before we buy any business, we carry out extensive research. It is imperative not to pay too much for it, and that the business does not run at a loss. We question what we are told and get a second opinion. If you view each investment property you buy as a business, you are less likely to make the mistake of buying an investment property for emotional reasons.

The second loan method

Another, and often preferred, method of borrowing more than 80 percent of a property's value is to get a second loan.

Banks usually have no hesitation in lending an investor 80 percent of a property's value. The loan is obviously considerably less than the value of the property, and the rent should cover most, if not all, of the loan repayments.

Mortgage insurance

The problem with loans above 80 percent of a property's value is that you must get mortgage insurance approval, and you cannot go through your financial report personally with the mortgage insurance company. However thoroughly you go through your report with the bank manager and however delighted the bank may be to lend you money, you still need the mortgage insurance company's approval.

This does not mean that it is futile to spend time with the bank manager and explain your financial report in detail. The happier the bank manager is to lend you money, the more they will try to get mortgage insurance approval for you.

Mortgage insurance is also expensive. The costs are calculated on the total loan amount, not just the amount over 80 percent of the property's value. Mortgage insurance costs start from 0.36 percent and go up to 1.96 percent of the loan amount, depending on the size of the loan and what percentage you want to borrow.

This can be exorbitant if you are borrowing only a little over 80 percent of the value. If, for instance, you want to buy a property for $400,000 and you need to borrow $350,000 (87.5 percent of $400,000), the cost of mortgage insurance is $4116.95, excluding government charges (mortgage insurance calculated at 1.17 percent of $350,000, source: NAB). If you borrowed $30,000 less, you would save the cost of mortgage insurance.

A calculated risk

One way to avoid mortgage insurance is to apply for a second loan to cover any extra funds you need over 80 percent of the property's value. Even if the second loan charges higher interest than your 80 percent bank loan, and as a result appears less attractive, it may be cheaper than mortgage insurance.

This means that if borrowing $350,000 to buy a property for $400,000, you can get an 80 percent loan for $320,000 and a second loan for $30,000. Even if the interest charged on the second loan is, for instance, 3 percent higher than your 80 percent loan, this extra cost only equates to $900 each year. After three years the interest will be $2,700.

If after 3 years the property has increased in value by more than 5 percent, you can re-finance and secure one new loan for 80 percent of the property's increased value. With this new loan you re-pay your two loans of $320,000 and $30,000. As a result, the second loan has cost an extra $2,700 in higher interest charges over 3 years. Mortgage insurance would cost $4116.95.

Keep it in context

Remember, you do not need to have this second higher-interest loan indefinitely. As soon as the property grows enough in value that a new 80 percent loan will repay two or more loans, you can re-finance. By doing this you can amalgamate your loans and better manage your finances.

Another important point is that the second loan is for a relatively small amount. Your first loan covers 80 percent of the amount you wish to borrow. The second is only to cover any funds needed above 80 percent. No one wants to pay higher interest than is absolutely necessary, but this extra cost is relatively minor, both in the context of the purchase and in the long run.

Investment properties should be neutrally or positively geared. Obviously, any extra interest charges can adversely affect this. Use different variables in your financial analysis to determine how interest rate fluctuations and the like can influence how the investment is geared in the future. Use conservative figures in your financial analysis to allow for any unexpected costs.

Remember, as soon as the property increases sufficiently in value you can re-finance your loans and remove any high-interest loans.

Equity benefits

Another benefit of having two loans is that you can treat them similarly to a split loan. I favour interest-only loans to keep my loan repayments as affordable as possible, keeping my investment portfolio neutrally or positively geared. With smaller second loans, you may chose to make lump sum payments of the principal, or make principal and interest repayments. If you do this you will repay these loans quicker, and as a result, you'll build equity in your property quicker.

Second mortgages are not readily available from all banks. Most first-tier banks only want the first mortgage on a property. However, second mortgages are readily available from almost all other types of financial institutions, including second-tier banks, building societies, community banks, and even solicitors who lend money on behalf of their clients. These lenders advertise regularly on television and in newspapers.

Although some leading banks may not promote second mortgages, I have received two loans from the same first-tier bank to settle a property. I explained that I wanted two loans to avoid mortgage insurance costs. This is the main benefit from two loans, but you also have more influence over whether they will be approved. You can meet personally with the bank manager and go through your financial report.

Sometimes it is better to get two loans, but you may have no choice if you cannot get mortgage insurance. It is important to keep your loans and their overall cost to you in perspective. To further emphasise this point I have shown two scenarios below:

First Scenario: Interest only home investment loan for $340,000 at 6.7 percent p.a. Total interest charged p.a. is $22,780.

Second Scenario: Interest only home investment loan for $320,000 at 6.7 percent p.a. Total interest charged p.a. is $21,440.

Personal loan for $20,000 at 10.9 percent p.a. Total interest charged p.a. is $2,180.

The second scenario will cost only $840 extra per annum in higher interest charges, but will also save the cost of mortgage insurance. When preparing a financial analysis, use different interest rates and scenarios to determine how much the property is really going to cost you.

Remember that for the second scenario, the property only has to increase in value by $20,000 for you to re-finance and repay the personal loan.

Think of what your goals are, and just like the costs for deposit bonds, keep expenses in perspective. If you are unwilling to consider two loans because it costs a little more, you may be unable to afford your investment property.

Interest

One of the largest fears people have about buying property is that interest rates may rise.

To give investors and home buyers peace of mind, you can fix the interest rate from 1 to 10 years, so that you know your expenses in advance. If after the first year your investment is positively geared, you can be fairly sure your investment will stay positively geared while the interest rate is fixed.

But what happens when the fixed interest rate expires? The options are to re-fix the interest rate, leave it on a variable rate, or sell the property. It is impossible to know the best option until the fixed interest rate terminates, because there are so many variables. As a general rule, if interest rates have increased during the period, your rent will also have increased.

During periods of low inflation and low interest rates, house prices usually increase. Because this market attracts more buyers, demand for rental properties lags. Tenants who previously rented a home look to buy, and more rental properties become available because more investors buy homes. As a result, rental vacancy rates go up and rents go down.

By contrast, when interest rates rise fewer people can afford to buy a property. This leads to higher rental demand, which leads to lower vacancy rates and higher rents. This cycle will go on indefinitely.

The most important thing about owning an investment property is servicing the debt, because if you service the debt the property will increase in value all by itself. Naturally, to service a debt you must be aware of any fluctuations that might occur in interest rates, and you must anticipate how this will affect your investment into the future.

Whatever happens in the future, you can always sell the property. Later in chapter 15, "Rules to Remember", I expand on this subject. If you decide to sell your property you need to allow for selling costs, which will be about 5 percent of the value of the property. 2–3 percent is for the agent's commission, 1–2 percent for marketing, and about $1000 for conveyancing and miscellaneous expenses.

Summary

- Before approaching banks to arrange finance for properties you have purchased, prepare the relevant financial reports.
- Leave time after purchasing to get an independent valuation. Collect evidence of positive indicators to support your case.
- Include details of existing investment properties in your financial report. Use colour brochures of your properties to add interest.
- Meet directly with a bank manager apply for a new loan that takes advantage of your increased equity demonstrated by the valuation. Send just one member of your syndicate to begin with.
- Meet with a second bank to keep your options open. Make sure you let this sec-

ond bank know you are meeting with their competition.

- Loans exceeding 80 percent of the value of the security require mortgage insurance approval.
- When looking for extra funds to settle a purchase, credit cards, friends, family members, bosses, and colleagues are all potential sources. Experience and past results will give you and your lenders confidence and help you raise money.
- It is possible to raise almost an unlimited amount of money for property bought at a genuine discount from market value where you can service the loan and other costs associated with the property.
- Treat every property you buy as a business: do extensive research, don't pay too much for it, and don't run it at a loss.
- Taking out a second loan to cover funds needed in excess of 80 percent of the purchased property's value can be an alternative to mortgage insurance. This second loan will be for a relatively small amount, and you don't have to keep it indefinitely.
- Don't worry that interest rates will rise. You can fix the interest rate for a period,

and when that period expires, your rent is likely to have increased and may cover higher interest. And whatever happens in the future, you can always sell.

14. Joint Ventures

Sometimes it is not possible or desirable to buy properties in bulk, or in a syndicate. If you are considering buying a property by yourself, it is still possible to receive a genuine discount off market value.

Properties in the early stages of a medium size development are often sold for less to encourage sales. However, the disadvantage to buying at this early stage is that the development may not proceed, due to poor sales. If there are a few properties left at the end of a development these may also be sold for less, either because marketing one or two properties is not cost-effective, or the developer may simply want to move on to the next project.

Vendors sell for many reasons, and these factors can also lead to properties selling for below their true market value. To take advantage of opportunities as they arise, you must carry out thorough research and become an expert on sales prices in a particular area. If you find a property you like, but you think is too expensive, make an offer anyway. It costs you nothing other than time, and unbeknownst to you the owner may have an urgent need to sell.

If you cannot afford the cost of a deposit bond or do not qualify for a bond, you need a joint venture partner.

Joint ventures are usually between two parties, each of whom is providing something the other party needs. You might have the time and knowledge to find properties at below market value, and the confidence and ability to negotiate the purchase of a property at a genuine discount price, but not the money or the assets required to get a deposit bond. A joint venture partner could secure and pay for a deposit bond, but may not have your real estate knowledge, ability or inclination to find the right investment property.

What you should know

In order to persuade a potential joint venture partner that you have found a suitable investment property, you need to prepare a mini financial report in the way I have described. Ideally it would include:

- An agreed purchase price
- Comparable sales evidence
- Rental estimates
- Financial analysis
- Independent valuation
- Depreciation schedule

The last two items are not absolutely essential.

If you cannot afford the cost of an independent valuation, you will need to use comparable sales evidence to convince your potential joint venture partner that you have negotiated the purchase of a property below its market value. You will still need an independent valuation later to satisfy the bank, but your joint venture partner may agree to pay for this as well as the deposit bond if you can reach a satisfactory joint venture agreement.

Likewise, it does not matter who pays for the depreciation schedule and other costs, provided that the person who is paying is compensated in some way through the joint venture agreement.

If you cannot afford a depreciation schedule but you still want a joint venture partner, leave the allowable depreciation total at zero dollars. If you do identify depreciable items at a later stage, you can claim these in your tax return. However, your main focus should be on securing investments that are positively geared *before* tax. Any allowable depreciation items will not affect this.

If you do not know what income your joint venture partner makes, make a conservative guess. Just like a depreciation schedule, a person's income has no bearing on how an investment is geared before tax. The financial analysis asks for a person's income to determine how the investment will be geared *after* tax.

If you underestimate a person's income, and the investment is still positively geared before and after tax, the correct income will not affect how the investment is geared, either before or after tax.

If, on the other hand, you overestimate your joint venture partner's income and later insert a lower figure in the financial analysis, it may affect how the investment is geared after tax.

For these reasons, it is not crucial that you have a depreciation schedule before you meet with your potential joint venture partner. Likewise, it is not mandatory to have an independent valuation when you agree in principle to a joint venture agreement. However, it is better to have an independent valuation before entering into a sale contract to purchase your investment property.

It is, however, crucial to have the first four items on the above list when meeting with a joint venture partner.

I have already explained how to collect rental estimates, comparable sales evidence and how to prepare a financial analysis.

The purchase price

The other crucial piece of information is a purchase price that the property owner has agreed to. Knowing that you cannot afford a deposit bond, you must proceed carefully when negotiating an acceptable purchase price, but there are ways you can protect yourself from making commitments you cannot meet.

The simplest way to avoid any problems is to keep your negotiations verbal. Usually, though, as negotiations draw to an end, the estate agent and owner will want you to sign a sale contract. To delay this, make it clear you will sign a contract but only after you reach a satisfactory agreement. Without an agreement, there is no need to waste anybody's time with unnecessary paper work.

If you agree on a satisfactory purchase price, meet any potential joint venture partners you have in mind, but be aware that if you delay signing the sale contracts too long the owner may sell their property to someone else.

If you do sign a sale contract before you have had time to finalise a joint venture agreement, you can include a clause in the Sale contract to this effect:

> This sale is subject to and conditional upon the purchaser obtaining a deposit bond, which shall be provided to satisfy the deposit requirements of this contract. This condition ends after 7 days from the date of this contract. If the purchaser cannot obtain a deposit bond within the time specified the purchaser may end this contract by informing the estate agent (or owner) in writing and if the contract is ended all monies paid must be refunded in full.

This condition gives you one week (or longer, depending on the time specified) to find a joint venture partner and secure a deposit bond using their assets. If you are unable to find a joint venture partner, and as a result you cannot secure a deposit bond, the sale contract can be terminated without becoming a liability.

Options

Another way to protect yourself is to use an option. An option gives the purchaser greater protection than the clause above, because it does not apply specifically to deposit bonds and allows the purchaser to end the sale contract for any reason.

Options are usually created by solicitors, and accordingly, they attract legal fees. Options also usually include a non-refundable cash payment, which is paid to the owner if they agree to the option.

An option is like having an extended cooling-off period, during which time the purchaser can contemplate whether they will buy the property. Because options offer the owner no guarantee that their property is sold, the owner usually receives a non-refundable cash payment to entice them to accept the option. The owner keeps this money whether the option holder decides to buy the property or not.

If the owner agrees to the option, the property is taken off the market. The option holder then has the exclusive right to purchase the property at the agreed price. Options are usually for periods longer than one week, and may last for months. Developers or speculators who want to carry out more extensive research before buying a property often use options. This research can take considerable time and money, and a prospective purchaser does not want to commit time and funds to a property without some reassurance that it will not be sold to another buyer.

A typical example of when an option may be used is a developer wanting to buy a multi-unit development site, but only if they can build high-density units. If the property is purchased with a six-month option, the developer can approach local council and other relevant authorities to seek permissions to develop. Usually, the longer the option lasts the more it will cost the developer, but it could cost a great deal more to buy the property and then discover that there are restrictions preventing a development.

Although there may be other ways to negotiate the purchase of a property and still have the time to find a joint venture partner, the techniques I have mentioned are the most common. Estate agents, in particular, are familiar with them, and as a result, if you use these methods you should not encounter much resistance.

Once you have agreed to a purchase price and prepared your mini financial report, meet with your potential joint venture partner and go through all the information. This meeting will be excellent practice, and a good opportunity to boost your confidence for similar meetings you will have with valuers and bank managers.

To persuade a joint venture partner to invest in the property, you need to convince them that the equity they will make from buying the property will be far more than what it will cost them. In fact, what you are selling to a potential joint venture partner is a business opportunity too good to miss.

For example, say you want to purchase an investment property for $330,000, and this property has been independently valued at $370,000. If your joint venture partner invests $2,500 for a deposit bond and an independent valuation, they will receive half of the investment property, and therefore half of the $40,000 equity. They effectively make $20,000 worth for only $2,500.

Ideally, both parties share equally all ongoing costs after the property is settled, and both parties have an equal share in the property. This ensures that when the investment property is sold, the profit is also shared equally.

The point you must emphasise to your joint venture partner is that although it may appear that they are providing the whole funds to settle the property, you expended time and energy searching for properties. You also spent money driving around inspecting properties to make this deal possible. If you both agree, you can jointly apply for a bank loan and share any ongoing costs after the property settles.

If you have found the right investment property, your out-of-pocket expenses after the property has settled should be nil or negligible. As I mentioned, this is the ideal.

Most homes are sold to couples who have a similar arrangement, even if it is not formally written down or referred to as a joint venture. However, you are not limited to joint venture agreements where both parties have an equal share in a property.

Alternatives to joint ventures

One burgeoning real estate business is buyer advocacy services. Buyer advocates work just like traditional estate agents—in fact most buyer advocates are former estate agents—but they work for the buyer, not the seller. Also like estate agents, buyer advocates work on a commission-only basis and charge a fee based upon the purchase price of a property.

Usually the commission fee charged is between 2–3 percent of the purchase price of the property. If you find a suitable investment property and an investor willing to buy it, you might decide to receive an advocacy fee for finding the property instead of forming a joint venture agreement. Verbally negotiating the purchase price of a property does not mean you have to sign the contracts to buy that property. You may prefer to make money from real estate without buying a single property.

Another alternative might be to find a joint venture partner who buys the property you have found solely in their name. You then enter into an agreement whereby you are entitled to a share of the profit if the property is sold in the future. Under this arrangement, you will not have to contribute to any costs relating to the property. An arrangement like this may suit people who do not want to apply for a bank loan, even with another person, for fear of being rejected.

As an example, if you negotiate the purchase a property for $330,000 and it is independently valued at $370,000, you might find a joint venture partner who prefers to buy the property solely in their name. You might agree to enter into a joint venture agreement that if the property is later sold for a figure over $330,000, you will be entitled to a percentage above that figure. There are no set rules on how you should structure this agreement. The nominated figure could be between $330,000 and $370,000, and the percentage you receive could vary between 1 percent and 50 percent.

It is important to remember that if your joint venture partner is the sole owner of the property, they will incur all costs when the property is sold. As I explained earlier in this book, the selling costs are generally around 5 percent of the property's value. Therefore, you might include in your joint venture agreement that you are entitled to a percentage of the profit after all selling costs have been deducted from the property's sale price.

Your joint venture partner may have no intention of ever selling the property. If this is the case, obviously you cannot use a sale price to determine how much money you will receive in the future. Instead, use an independent valuer's assessment of the property's value after a predetermined time frame. Based upon this independent valuation, your joint venture partner should pay you your entitlement under your joint venture agreement and the agreement is then terminated.

If your joint venture partner does not have the funds to pay you, they can re-finance the property to raise the money required.

Whether a joint venture entitles both parties to an equal share in a property or not, if you can find a property below its true market value and you can clearly demonstrate this to a purchaser, you can make money from real estate. The type and number of joint venture agreements you can make are endless. The only limit is your imagination.

Summary

- A joint venture partnership can be a good alternative to deposit bonds
- The financing partner needs to feel that the equity will repay their investment
- The depreciation schedule, and your partner's income, do not affect gearing before tax, only after tax
- Agree on a purchase price and protect yourself, either contractually or by using an option
- Alternatives include buyer advocacy commissions, or a joint venture partnership buying in only one person's name

15. Top Ten Rules to Remember

Each of us grows up with a set of rules that we believe is true and sacred. Most of these come from our parents and family at a young age. Others we forge from our own life experiences. Many of these rules we have held for so long that we no longer know where they came from, and we rarely review them to see if they still apply.

One of the rules I believed was "do not rent a home because rent money is dead money", simply because I had heard it so many times. It was only very recently that I thought about this saying and challenged it.

Here are the top ten rules I believe are crucial to ensure success, but I do encourage readers to challenge these rules and add to or modify them.

These rules are from my personal experiences. Some may seem obvious to some readers, while other readers may feel that I have omitted a more important rule. I learn a little more with every new property I purchase, and I will add to my list of rules as I go. I encourage readers to do the same.

1. Question those long-held beliefs

These are often things like "rent money is dead money", "your parents know best", "your home is your best investment", "be careful with your money and don't over spend", "debt is bad", "save your money for a rainy day", "some people are born lucky", or "you need money to make money". I am not passing judgment on these enduring and well-known sayings, however I suggest that you review such sayings and decide for yourself whether they are true or false.

2. Listen and take advice from people who have achieved what you want to achieve

The world is full of critics, and some of these may be people close to you. If you succeed, you will expose their failings and insecurities. Do not listen or let them prevent you from starting your journey. Typically, the loudest nay-sayers are people who are too timid to have tried themselves. If you listen to these people, a doubt will grow until you are incapable of acting because of other people's fears. In my experience, people who have achieved what you want to achieve are happy to share their success. They are generally gracious and humble.

They are secure in the knowledge that they have made it, and they don't mind helping you get there too.

3. You are capable of anything you set your mind to

This may sound trite, but it is worth repeating. You will face many hurdles and some failures, but with self-belief and perseverance you can overcome these obstacles. A syndicate can be particularly helpful when problems arise. In a syndicate you can brainstorm any problems, and you may be surprised how many different ideas are forthcoming and how creative some of the suggestions may be. For every potentially disastrous problem you will face, there is a solution. When the obvious does not work, remember necessity can drive people to ingenious solutions.

4. Expect the worst

This does not mean that you should become a pessimist. However, be aware that obstacles can present themselves. Try to think of potential problems ahead of time, and have back-up plans ready. As soon as you start putting your second plan into action, start thinking about a third alternative. The difference between a pessimist and being prepared for the worst-case scenario is that a pessimist believes nothing will work. An optimist believes that although you might face challenges along the way, with perseverance you can reach your goals. When I started I faced a number of hurdles. My inspiration came from the stories I read about battlers who started with very little but managed to buy large investment portfolios, and are now enjoying their lives to the fullest. Since these people could do it, I believed there must be a way of overcoming my own obstacles. Whenever you come to a potential problem, get advice from people who have achieved what you want to achieve, and remember that there must be a solution. After all, buying investment properties is not like flying to the moon. Thousands of ordinary people have done it before you.

5. Property prices will always go up

This is not completely true, but almost completely. To illustrate this point, I have provided lists of the median property prices for the cities of Melbourne and Sydney over the past 50 years, using data from the Australian Bureau of Statistics and BIS Shrapnel. These appear in the appendix at the very end of this book.

The lists show that in the past 50 years, the median house price has fallen only 7 times in Melbourne and 8 times in Sydney. Similar results have been recorded for the other Australian capital cities. When the median house price did fall, the largest price decrease recorded in a single year for Melbourne was 4.7 percent, and in Sydney the largest recorded fall was 5.2 percent. The total number of years the median price fell in Melbourne and Sydney over the past 50 years, was 15 years. This means that over the past 50 years, there was a greater than 85 percent chance that the median price in a particular year increased or at least remained the same. An 85 percent chance that a property would increase in value after a year are excellent odds. That is why banks and other financial institutions are prepared to lend purchasers up to 95 percent to buy a property. By contrast, banks will only lend investors 50 percent to buy shares in their own bank. Banks accept that properties are a safer investment than their own shares.

The figures also show that properties can decrease in value, and undoubtedly there will be years when prices will fall. If, however, you are able to buy a property with a genuine discount of just 5 percent below market value, the past 50 years have shown that it is unlikely that the value of your property will ever fall below the price you paid.

The most important message from the past 50 years is *service your mortgage.* If you do this, the property will increase in value all by itself. Many investors will procrastinate about buying a property because they believe the market has reached its peak and tougher times are ahead.

I believe there is no better time to buy a property than now, provided you buy the right property and you can service the debt. There will always be some people who think the market is about to dip. In fact, in the past 50 years the market in Melbourne and Sydney has not fallen by more than 5.2 percent in any year. The most average home in the most average suburb increased from around $8,500 in 1960 to almost $500,000 in Melbourne and over $600,000 in Sydney in 2010. During this period, even the most average properties almost doubled in value every ten years.

It is hard to imagine that in the next ten years property prices could double, but if you asked your parents or grandparents whether they thought an average home would now sell for $500,000, they would give you a resounding no. Our parents and grandparents could give us an infinite list of homes they should have bought ten years ago for prices we can now only dream of.

Don't be like so many people who regret what they have not done. If we could travel back in time and show a 1960 homeowner that their property would be worth almost $500,000 in 2010, they would have bought every property possible, even if they were $1,000 or $2,000 overpriced, and they would have done everything possible to buy them.

Therefore, my advice to anyone who wants to sell their investment property in a depressed market is to hold on. If you cannot afford to hold onto your investment, then do not be greedy. Be satisfied to sell your investment property in a depressed market for a profit. As an estate agent, I have seen numerous sellers decline an offer in the hope of selling their home for 1–2 percent more, only to chase the market down and ultimately sell the property for less than they were initially offered. Making a profit when the market is down it is certainly better than making a loss.

Homeowners often want to sell their home when the market is buoyant, because they will achieve a higher price which gives them an inflated feeling of wealth. My advice, if you are thinking of selling your home to upgrade, is to sell and buy in a depressed market. The savings can be considerable.

Estate agents' commission and government stamp duty are calculated as a percentage of the property's value. Therefore, the lower the price for the home you are buying, the less you pay for stamp duty. Likewise, the lower you sell your home for, the less you pay an estate agent. The added benefit in a depressed market is that you can also negotiate lower commission fees because estate agents are more desperate for business.

The other reason why homeowners upgrading should sell in a depressed market is that the home they are upgrading to will most likely fall further in price than their own home. As a general rule, the more expensive a property is, the more that property will fall in value in a depressed market (when expressed as a percentage). There are always buyers in the lower-priced market who can afford and genuinely need a home, but buyers in the upper market usually become comparatively scarce as some high-flyers become aware that they have over-committed financially during the good times. If, for instance you are selling your home, which was worth $300,000, for $250,000 in a depressed market, there may be no better time to pick up that million-dollar mansion for around $800,000, or perhaps indulge yourself and pick up the two million-dollar mansion for around $1.5 million. You may miss out on $50,000, but you can potentially save hundreds of thousands, which means a smaller mortgage and, again, lower costs.

6. *Appear confident and relaxed when negotiating.*

This may sound easy, but some people become extremely nervous when they are negotiating, particularly if they are unfamiliar with what is involved. Although you want to appear confident, you should not be aggressive or arrogant. Listen to what the other side say and then respond to their comments point by point before making your own. Speak clearly and concisely. "Ums" and "ahs" give the impression that you are indecisive and unsure. Try to sound even and calm. Expressive vocal inflections can appear overly emotional. Do not rush what you say. Use pauses. A pause before you speak can be very powerful, and will ensure the other party is listening. Be courteous and wait for them to finish speaking before you respond. If you do this they will reciprocate. If one person raises their voice, usually the other person will do the same until you are both yelling, and your negotiations will end disappointingly.

You do not want to give the impression that you are intimidated, so act relaxed. Begin with a clear picture in your mind of what your best result would be, and what you would consider a satisfactory result. If you start any negotiation with only one acceptable result you might find the negotiations end quickly because you have no flexibility.

It is important to develop good negotiation skills because, if you are buying an investment property in the way I have described in this book, you will need to negotiate with valuers, estate agents, rental property managers, bank managers, quantity surveyors, developers, and perhaps even prospective tenants. Some of these people will be excellent negotiators, and if you are not comfortable with negotiating, the process may seem daunting. If you seem timid or nervous it is easy for the other party to decline any requests you make. It may help to appear bored. Bored people automatically use more pauses when speaking, and this will give the impression that you have carefully considered your argument and that it is important. Your voice will be more monotone, so that you seem relaxed. A bored, relaxed pose will also give the other party the impression that what you are offering them is more important or valuable than what they are giving you in return.

7. Carry out extensive research.

The real estate market is constantly changing. Every sale, whether big or small, can change the market in some way. For each sale there is a pool of buyers who are aware of the result, and will use this information to influence how much they will offer for the next property. Every sale, to some degree, changes a buyer's expectations of what will happen to the real estate market in the immediate future. Sales occur every day, and it is impossible for estate agents and valuers to keep abreast of every result. A buyer cannot do so either. However, it is still vital to carry out extensive research and to use your knowledge of the real estate market to your advantage.

I have found that valuers have the least knowledge of particular areas, because they provide valuations over vast areas and usually only have a broad overview of the real estate market. Estate agents generally have good local knowledge, however their knowledge is usually confined to the properties they have sold or are selling. Buyers, on the other hand, often have the best local knowledge of all, because they inspect all the homes for sale in a particular area. These buyers will often build rapport with different estate agents from different agencies. That is why it is important to carry out extensive research, so that when you find a property you want to buy you can convince the estate agent what it is worth and negotiate a better purchase price.

Likewise, you can use your superior knowledge of the local market to persuade the valuer that you have purchased the property for a price below its true market value. I believe that before you buy any property it is vital to find sales evidence dating back six months, as well as researching more recent sales results and current properties for sale. Doing this means you are less likely to be influenced by anomalies. This process may take weeks of research in a particular area, but there is no such thing as too much research. The more you know, the better prepared you will be.

8. Don't be miserly.

This certainly does not mean you should be careless with your money. The underlying importance of this rule is to recognise when you need professional advice or assistance and get it, even if it means extra expense.

You may be able to save a few hundred dollars if, for instance, you prepare your own depreciation schedule and do not use a quantity surveyor. However, if you do not have the necessary expertise you could overlook a tax deductible item which could cost you thousands, and not just in the first year as you can continue using the same depreciation schedule for many years. The same applies to accountants and other professionals. A cheaper accountant may not specialise in property matters and may miss tax claims you are entitled to.

Therefore, if you need expert advice, check that the person you are using really is an expert. Even if it costs a little extra to use someone who is better qualified and experienced, you should use them because they will get you the maximum benefits you are entitled to. Remember, costs for professional services relating to your investment property are tax deductible, so really the difference in cost between two accountants, or two quantity surveyors, or two rental property managers may not be as great as you think.

There is also no long-term benefit in not paying for any help you might receive along the way from family and friends. If you need friendly advice from someone who has achieved what you are aspiring to, or financial assistance from family or friends, and you do not adequately acknowledge or thank these people, you may not receive any further help in the future. These people may not ask for acknowledgement or payment, but they are usually very appreciative. If you feel uncomfortable giving someone money, give them a gift voucher, or a dinner voucher, or an overnight stay in a nice hotel or bed-and-breakfast. They will generally be there for you in the future. Remember that without these people's help you might not reach your goals, so keep your costs in perspective. If someone gives you financial assistance and, to show your gratitude, you pay for them to stay in a classy hotel, it might be the best long-term investment you ever make.

9. Buying investment properties is a business, so treat it as one.

If you view each new property as a business, you will be less emotional and able to focus on each task more effectively. There are an almost unlimited number of business opportunities available and some people are in the business of buying and selling these on a regular basis. If you buy a business and it does not work out or reach your expectations, you sell it and buy another until you find what you are looking for. The same applies to investment properties. To emphasise this I believe that it is best, even if it seems trivial, to dress in a business suit. If you dress and act like a professional investor, you will be treated like a professional investor.

10. Have clearly defined goals.

Numerous books and seminars tell you how to set goals. Setting goals is crucial. Many people think about buying investment properties, but let the pressures of daily life prevent them. This is particularly important if you have a spouse. You need to discuss and set goals together, and make the time to achieve them. Looking for suitable properties can be demanding, particularly on weekends when most people want to enjoy their leisure time. However your long-term goal should be to create more leisure time by acquiring an investment portfolio, which will provide you with a passive income in the future. Short-term pain is enough to stifle the dreams and aspirations of some people. However, with clearly defined goals you will overcome the short-term obstacles because you will remain focused on the long-term gains.

Each person will set different goals, and different time frames to achieve them. However, you should not be influenced by other people's goals. Set realistic goals and stick to them. When you reach your goals, set new ones. After you have acquired a property portfolio your new goal may not be about purchasing more investment properties. It might be about enjoying life and spending more time with family. Whatever your goals are, when you reach them take the time to reflect on what you have achieved and how you did it, and then think about what you want from life. If you do this you will not mistake the means for the end.

Summary

- Question long-held beliefs
- Take advice from people who've done it before
- You are capable of anything
- Plan for failures
- Property prices will always go up, so buy now and service your mortgage
- Appear confident and relaxed when negotiating
- Do your research
- Invest in good advice
- Be professional and businesslike
- Have clearly defined goals

16. Conclusion

I decided to write this book because after reading several books and attending numerous seminars about buying investment properties, I naively thought it would be easy to build my own investment portfolio if I could just get started. I thought banks and other lending institutions would throw money at me and do their utmost to make me their new customer.

Unfortunately, the books I read and the seminars I attended often did not inform me where to start, let alone what to do when I encountered obstacles.

I do not want to appear critical of the books I have read or seminars I attended. On the contrary, I learnt something beneficial from every book and seminar. At the very least I had important information reinforced. This accumulation of information eventually gave me the confidence to buy my own investment properties.

Extensive research is vital when choosing suitable investment properties, and not just on which property to buy. You should also learn as much as possible about investment properties in general and everything related to the subject. Read newspaper articles, magazines, and books, and attend seminars which deal with this topic.

I also do not want to give the impression that it is difficult to buy investment properties. I have no doubt some readers will find it far easier to buy investment properties than I have.

I decided to write this book to give a frank account of what some people may experience along the way. Please do not be discouraged. I have found the whole experience rewarding and in the main, extremely enjoyable. There is an undeniable feeling of achievement when you have reached your goals and you can set yourself new challenges.

I hope that readers will be better prepared than I was and will be able to avoid some of the mistakes I made.

I also hope readers will be inspired to buy their own investment properties and know how to start.

After buying my own properties, I now truly believe that almost anyone can buy investment properties.

The steps I describe in this book enabled me to secure thirteen properties in the first twelve months. The pace at which each reader will acquire properties will depend on their personal circumstances. However, if you put the time and energy required into researching the real estate market and finding suitable properties, I believe you can set almost any pace you like.

New homes are listed for sale every day, and any one of these could be your new investment property. As I explained earlier in this book, if you are able to service your loan, the property will grow in value all by itself. As each year passes it should get easier and easier to service your loans and hold onto your investments.

The reason is that for each property your debt is not growing, and the property's value is probably increasing. If you have fixed the interest rate on your loan, your expenses should remain about the same, but the rental income your investment generates should increase.

As I have shown, over the past fifty years property prices have seldom decreased. By contrast, rental returns (when expressed as a percentage) seem to fluctuate fairly regularly. This is usually because home prices increase faster than rents. Rents are not usually as volatile as house prices and will usually increase steadily, at least in line with inflation, whereas at times house prices increase rapidly.

In real terms, rents rarely decrease.

Assuming that your investment will take care of itself in the long-term, it is imperative to get the short-term right. More things can potentially go wrong in the short-term.

Because of this, I have focused on how to buy an investment property and what qualities you should look for. If you buy the right property for the right price, and things do not work out or your personal circumstances change, you can always sell it.

If you sell your investment property shortly after you bought it, the amount of profit you make will be largely determined by the size of the discount you were able to negotiate. If you start right, generally the future will take care of itself.

The first year is the most difficult. There may be out-of-pocket expenses such as a telephone connection fee or fittings, or there may be a vacancy between settlement and tenancy. During this period, the investment obviously generates no income, but you are still servicing the loan. Real estate agencies take a letting fee, usually equivalent to two weeks' rent. There are automatic deductions from your bank account to service the loan.

I have always found that after the first year, things get easier, particularly after I have had each property for a full tax year. I always look forward to tax time, because when my accountant prepares my tax return I receive a profit and loss statement for each property. I can see in real dollars and cents what my investments have made or cost before tax and after tax.

This information is vital for me to plan strategies and set targets. Even if the real estate market becomes slightly depressed and my investments do not grow in value as fast as I had hoped, my rent keeps paying my loans, and I know that better times are ahead.

Appendix

The following four tables show a history of median house price growth in Melbourne and Sydney from 1960 to 2010, to demonstrate rule number 5 from chapter 15: "Property prices will always go up." The data presented in these tables was collected as part of my real estate and property investment practices over the course of several years, and includes data from the Australian Bureau of Statistics as well as a range of other sources.

Sydney house price growth 1960–1985

Year	Median price ($)	Annual growth (%)
1960	8,500	3.6
1961	8,800	3.5
1962	10,000	13.6
1963	10,500	5.0
1964	11,900	13.3
1965	11,800	−0.85
1966	12,600	6.7
1967	13,400	6.3
1968	14,800	10.4
1969	16,200	9.5
1970	18,500	14.2
1971	20,600	11.3
1972	23,700	15.0
1973	26,400	11.4
1974	33,000	25.0
1975	33,800	2.4
1976	37,300	10.3
1977	39,400	5.6
1978	45,800	16.2
1979	54,800	19.6
1980	69,700	27.1
1981	84,700	21.5
1982	84,300	−0.47
1983	82,900	−1.6
1984	79,400	−4.2
1985	85,200	7.3

Sydney house price growth 1986–2010

Year	Median price ($)	Annual growth (%)
1986	90,600	6.3
1987	92,100	1.6
1988	117,600	27.7
1989	182,300	55.0
1990	181,000	−0.38
1991	171,700	−5.2
1992	176,000	2.5
1993	180,000	2.2
1994	194,000	7.7
1994	194,000	7.7
1995	202,000	4.1
1996	210,000	3.9
1997	230,000	9.5
1998	260,000	13
1999	280,000	7.6
2000	318,000	13.6
2001	354,000	11.3
2002	393,500	11.1
2003	460,000	16.9
2004	498,000	8.3
2005	500,000	0.4
2006	495,000	−1
2007	512,300	3.5
2008	517,000	1
2009	490,000	−5.2
2010	612,000	24.9

Melbourne house price growth 1960–1985

Year	Median price ($)	Annual growth (%)
1960	8,300	3.8
1961	8,700	4.8
1962	8,500	−2.3
1963	8,100	−4.7
1964	8,800	8.6
1965	9,400	6.8
1966	9,700	3.2
1967	9,400	−3.1
1968	10,500	11.7
1969	11,400	8.6
1970	11,800	3.5
1971	12,100	2.5
1972	14,500	19.8
1973	19,800	36.6
1974	25,800	30.3
1975	27,800	7.8
1976	35,600	28.1
1977	38,600	8.4
1978	41,300	7.0
1979	45,000	9.0
1980	44,800	−0.4
1981	55,600	24.1
1982	57,600	3.6
1983	59,400	3.1
1984	69,300	16.7
1985	80,200	15.7

Melbourne house price growth 1986–2010

Year	Median price ($)	Annual growth (%)
1986	85,500	6.6
1987	97,000	13.5
1988	114,000	17.5
1989	130,000	14.0
1990	147,000	13.1
1991	142,000	−3.4
1992	136,000	−4.2
1993	145,000	6.6
1994	146,000	0.7
1994	145,000	−0.7
1995	153,000	5.5
1996	170,000	11.1
1997	198,000	16.5
1998	226,000	14.1
1999	236,000	4.4
2000	247,000	4.6
2001	260,000	5.2
2002	287,500	10.5
2003	307,500	7
2004	320,000	4
2005	345,000	7.8
2006	362,000	4.9
2007	400,000	10.5
2008	400,000	0
2009	500,000	25
2010	612,000	24.9

Connect with the author online

Mark Reister

Website
professionalsshepparton.com.au

www.ingramcontent.com/pod-product-compliance
Lightning Source LLC
Chambersburg PA
CBHW031952170526
45157CB00002B/463